Islam & Economics

A Primer on Markets, Morality, and Justice

To Gabriel Geagea,

I hope you enjoy reading it.

Ali Salman

23/06/22

Grand Rapids

Islam
& Economics

*A Primer on
Markets,
Morality, and
Justice*

Ali Salman

Foreword by Shaykh Abdullah bin Hamid Ali

ACTON INSTITUTE

ISBN 978-1-880595-46-6 (paperback)
ISBN (ebook) 978-1-880595-40-4

ACTON INSTITUTE
98 E. Fulton
Grand Rapids, Michigan 49503
616.454.3080
www.acton.org

Interior composition by Judy Schafer
Cover design by Peter Ho

Believers, when you are summoned to Friday prayers, hasten to the remembrance of God and cease your trading. That would be best for you, if you but knew it. Then, when the prayers are ended, disperse and go your ways in quest of God's bounty. Remember God always, so that you may prosper.

—Qur'an 62:9–10

Muhammad gave his community along with a new religion a framework for its economy. Muhammad's economic policy promoted entrepreneurial initiative, efficient distribution of resources, and wealth creation, a framework for creating wealth that lasted centuries.

—Benedikt Koehler
Early Islam and the Birth of Capitalism

A Selection of the Prophet Muhammad's Sayings

Your lives and your properties are forbidden to one another until you meet your Lord.

Water, fire and grass belong to community.

The servants are the servants of Allah, the land is the land of Allah and who revives dead land, it is for him.

God is the taker and the disposer, the provider, and the controller of prices. I hope that when I meet Him none of you will have a claim against me for an injury concerning life and property.

The one who hoards with the intention of pushing prices higher for the Muslims is a transgressor.

The believer is one whom the people entrust with their money and lives.

Trade is by mutual consent unless they differ; if they are honest and clear their trade is blessed, but if they are untruthful and unclear the blessing is removed.

CONTENTS

Foreword by Abdullah bin Hamid Ali   *xi*

Acknowledgments   *xxxiii*

Introduction   1

1. Islam, Markets, Morality, and Justice   7

2. Principles of the Islamic Economic Framework   11

    2.1. Principle of Ownership   13

    2.2. Principle of Wealth Creation   24

    2.3. Principle of Wealth Circulation   28

3. Institutional Tenets of the Islamic Economic Framework   33

    3.1. Price Freedom   33

    3.2. Free Trade   43

    3.3. Market Regulations   45

    3.4. Gold, Fiat Currency, and Central Banking   56

    3.5. *Riba* and an Islamic Alternative   63

    3.6. Islamic Fiscal Policy   71

    3.7. *Waqf*—Social Protection of People by People   80

    3.8. Law of Inheritance   83

4. Islamic Economic Framework: Historical Romance or Practical Prescription?   87

Appendix 1: Evolution of Islamic Economics   91

Appendix 2: Islam and Capitalism—Mawdudi Revisited   105

Bibliography   115

FOREWORD

ISLAM AND THE BOUNDARIES OF ECONOMIC FREEDOM

Suq is the Arabic *word* for "marketplace." It derives from the verb *saqa*, which means to steer someone or something in a particular direction or to a certain destination, as in "the shepherd steered the cattle to pasture" (*saqa al-ra'i al-an'am ila al-kala'*). The subjects of a kingdom are called *suqah*, from the same root. While both cattle and the subjects of a monarch possess limited control over their material destinies, they retain the will to resist strictures placed on them though generally choosing to remain compliant. This will or freedom to show indifference to commands is the faculty of choice, or what the Arabs refer to as *ikhtiyar*. Choice, however, is merely one crucial element for independent, responsible action, for without freedom of movement and opportunity to effectuate one's choices, the pursuit of happiness has little meaning in the lives of people. This ability to move freely as one wishes—or what postmodernists refer to as "agency"—corresponds to the Arabic word *hurriyah*.

The opposite of *hurriyah* is *riqq*, "bondage." Bondage has degrees. And a person's dignity is largely connected to the extent of their freedom. The lowest degree of *hurriyah* is for one not to be a slave. Its highest and noblest degree is the ability to break free of the material conditions that undermine one's overall happiness. If applied in the moral realm, the freest of people are those who gain mastery over their emotions and passions. In the words of the Egyptian sage, "You are free of what from which your hope is detached and a slave to the things you covet" (Al-Sakandari, aphorism no. 62).[1] In another aphorism he says, "You never love a thing except that you become its slave. And, He [God] does not like, to other than Him, for you to be a slave" (Al-Sakandari, aphorism no. 210).[2]

That both (directed) choice and (bounded) freedom influence the trade decisions of human beings implies that markets have, perhaps, always generally operated, at least in the Arab world, according to a de facto structure of free enterprise (cattle proceed) and the occasional intervention of a regulatory authority (shepherd steers). As the subjects of a kingdom may be persuaded by threat of force and a theory of divine right to reinforce monarchial norms, cattle are steered by sticks and carrots to continue their trek to their owner's intended destination. To be clear, markets thrive to the extent that buyers and sellers are not barred from consenting to trade on their own terms. But no amount of self-regulation can guarantee the absence of fraud and economic exploitation. For this reason, government must play, on the one hand, a decisive role in ensuring that greed does not have a paralyzing effect on markets, thereby leading to their collapse and with it the collapse of human flourishing. On the other hand, governments must also not become so intrusive into market affairs that the creative impulses and enthusiasm for greater profits of traders are not killed.

As Muslim societies attempted to shake free of the yoke of European colonization, they began to proffer their own theo-

---

[1] Ahmad b. 'Ata Allah al-Sakandari, *Al-Hikam Al-'Ata'iyyah* (Damascus: Hasan Al-Samahi Suwaydan, 1997), 23.

[2] Al-Sakandari, *Al-Hikam Al-'Ata'iyyah*, 50.

ries of economic well-being influenced by their understandings of Islam and comparisons with dominant Western theories. During the heyday of the Soviet Union that directly challenged Western European and American dominance, the macroeconomic options for Muslim nations were rather simple—either capitalism or socialism. Islamic reformers, however, probed the Islamic tradition in search of principles on which an original political economy could be constructed.[3] Rather, the more that Muslim reformers resisted the assertation of Western civilizational superiority, they opted to advance counter theories and models of many organic human social institutions, including government and economic systems. The "Islamic finance" and "Shariah compliant" sector that flourishes today can be seen as the most recent example of this phenomenon inasmuch as it is a "prohibition-oriented" enterprise operating on the presumption of the illegality of novel business transactions that do not originate in Muslim circles.[4]

If the West celebrates progress, the Muslim reaction has largely been a celebration of tradition in one form or another. For this reason, Muslim scholars and reformists have often reached back into the past for guidance and analogues to accommodate transactions whose precursors go back to Europe or to delegitimize any that appear to clash with classical Muslim legal understanding—that is, unless there is a precedent in at

---

[3] One of those reformers was the subcontinent writer, scholar, public intellectual, and politician Maulana Sayyid Abul A'la Mawdudi (d. 1979), who had significant influence on economic thought in Pakistan and on the Muslim world. In 1969 Mawdudi wrote his original Urdu work on economics, *Ma'āshiyyāt-i Islām*, which was later translated into English under the title *First Principles of Islamic Economics*, ed. Khurshid Ahmad, trans. Ahmad Imam Shafaq Hashemi (Markfield, UK: Islamic Foundation, 2011).

[4] The Egyptian economist Mahmoud A. El-Gamal characterizes contemporary Islamic financing as a "form" and "prohibition-oriented" finance in his book *Islamic Finance: Law, Economics, and Practice* (Cambridge: Cambridge University Press, 2006).

least one of the surviving legal schools. Contemporary jurists place themselves in a moral quandary in light of their adoption of legal eclecticism (*talfiq*), arbitrary intermural dispensations (*tatabbu' al-rukhas*), and legal ruses (*hiyal*) to validate transactions under legal dispute in classical jurisprudence. Though there is some historical disagreement, many of these same jurists generally describe this practice to junior and nonjurists as unlawful since it constitutes "whimsical decision making" (*ittiba' al-hawa*), which is condemned repeatedly by the Qur'an.[5]

While many jurists adopt this "jurisprudence of accommodation" approach to contemporary challenges in the areas of economics and finance, few have ventured to recreate the conditions under which a presumed "Islamic" economic system actually flourished, an order whose foundation is believed to be sound, reliable currency. Such a task has been proven extremely difficult, if not impossible, when one considers the 2014 decision by Shaykh Dr. Abdalqadir as-Sufi[6] and his Al-Murabitun movement to abandon the effort to reconstitute Islamic currency or the gold dinar and silver dirham. As-Sufi's declaration indicated that the compromise was too great since one still was required under Western currency exchanges to evaluate gold

---

[5] For an exposition of the different views on legal eclecticism and arbitrary intermural dispensations, see Muhammad Amno Al-Butibi, "Al-Maqbul Wa al-Mardud Min Tatabbu'i al-Rukhas Wa al-Talfiq Bayna al-Madhahib" [in Arabic], *Majallah al-Madhhab al-Maliki* (2006): 61–103.

[6] Shaykh Dr. Abdalqadir as-Sufi, formerly Ian Dallas, is a highly influential Scottish Muslim who converted to Islam in 1967 in Fes, Morocco. He is a Sufi and founder of the Murabitun World Movement, which has communities in several countries, with Spain being regarded as its heartland. This movement has focused considerably on the restoration of *zakat* as a cornerstone of a strong Muslim government economy, arguing for the Islamic illicitness of fiat currency and the importance of restoring the gold and silver standards to the world economic system. The movement can be considered anticapitalist in its orientation, although not necessarily pro-socialist. In 2014, however, As-Sufi abandoned the effort to restore the gold dinar and silver dirham.

according to Western standards.[7] In other words, the harsh reality had set in that one cannot break free of Western economic hegemony as long as the West determines the value of gold and as long as fiat currency is given as an equal substitute for it, which undermines an integral part of the Al-Murabitun argument, which is that fiat currency's value is nothing different from wastepaper. If so, this would mean that an illicit transaction happens every time a Muslim exchanges gold for paper money, since it is not lawful to exchange something of value for another thing that has no value at all.

With the increased participation in politics in Western countries today—and especially in light of current debates around the relative value of socialist vis-à-vis capitalistic policies—Muslims find themselves once again faced with a choice between socialism and capitalism. Or, rather, it is between synthesizing

---

[7] Shaykh Abdalqadir as-Sufi says,

> Thus a newer and wider method must be adopted on a global scale PRIOR to the return of a local Halal functioning community which restores Islam by the door of Zakat.
>
> Men must begin to trade and exchange, hand to hand, and transfer across distance without recourse to the financial instruments and institutions of capitalism.
>
> Therefore, to that constructive future activity I call Muslims to begin a post-usury culture.
>
> So, I now dis-associate myself from all activity involving the Islamic gold dinar and silver dirham.
>
> I call on an end to its new institutions and productivity. The defence mechanisms of today's late capitalism and its crisis management surrounding the buying, moving and minting of gold have surrounded it with prohibitive pricing and taxation.
>
> It is time to move beyond it. This is capitalism's pyrrhic victory. Ahead lies vast expansion for the post-terrorist and post-political stage of Muslim growth.

Shaykh Dr. Abdalqadir as-Sufi, "The Islamic Dinar—A Way-Stage Passed," Shaykh Dr. Abdalqadir as-Sufi (website), February 11, 2014, https://shaykhabdalqadir.com/2014/02/11/the-islamic-dinar-a-way-stage-passed/.

the two and preferring one over the other. Naturally, talk of more than 50 percent of the world's wealth being owned by 1 percent of the world's population, the steady rise and gross disparities in the salaries of CEOs and regular employees over the past century, corporate welfare, patenting of seeds and monopolization of food goods, and major tax breaks for the rich are more than a few good reasons to see why socialist wealth reallocations are appealing to so many people as opposed to capitalism, which is maligned as a grossly inhumane economic system that requires dismantling. If our taxes can be allocated for welfare on Wall Street, why can they not be used for Main Street?

On the other hand, what can be said about the advantages of the rich? Is there sufficient evidence that their affluence is always the direct result of exploitation of vulnerable populations living under conditions that force them to compromise against their greater interests? Or do most people simply make decisions based on the basic laws of supply and demand, leading them to buy the things they like and want? Should a corporation be held criminally or civically liable for providing a customer the opportunity to buy a desired good or a job with an acceptable salary? Is it a moral flaw of the corporation or business if consumers like their product, spend their money with them, or even develop an unhealthy attachment to goods offered? Is justice done to a businessperson who has exerted great effort on education, persevering and planning for his or her economic future and developing unique ideas to get ahead, when government usurps and reallocates—through high taxes—hard-earned profits for public benefit simply because others think they deserve to have a share in wealth they had no hand in creating? And what role do nihilism, hedonism, and atheism play in the breakdown of societal cohesion and compassionate economic practices?

The Qur'an says, "O you who believe! Eat not up your property among yourselves in vanities; But let there be among you tariff and trade by mutual good will" (4:29).[8] In other words, while exploitation is unequivocally condemned, the transfer of goods built on mutual consent is praised. One may add that this holds true even if it leads the seller to become rich as long as the buyer is satisfied with the goods being offered. But isn't eating up "property among yourselves in vanities" a two-way street? Should it not be the right of consumers to devour the private wealth of the affluent without exchanging something of value in the same way that the affluent should not be allowed to exploit consumers without offering something of desired value as well? The 2008 financial collapse cannot be solely blamed on corporate greed. If greed prevails on Wall Street, are we to assume that the members of Main Street lack this basic human impulse?

DOES ISLAM FAVOR A FREE MARKET?

The Qur'an says,

> Those who hoard up gold and silver and do not spend it in the way of God, give them tidings of a painful chastisement, on the day they will be heated in the fire of Hell and used to brand their foreheads, sides, and backs. This is what you hoarded up for yourselves. So, taste what you were hoarding up. (9:34–35)[9]

These verses of the Qur'an have multiple implications, including that economic activity is not completely divorced from religious concern. It forbids hoarding gold and silver while suggesting that there are appropriate ways and places where they are to be spent. This is taken from the expression "and do

---

[8] Ali, Abdullah Yusuf, *Modern English Translation of the Holy Qur'an: Meanings and Commentary* (Jeddah: Dar al-Qiblah Co. for Islamic Literature, 1998), 165.

[9] All quotations from the Qur'an and hadith translations in this foreword are my own unless otherwise specified.

not spend it in the way of God." As in an earlier verse (4:29), this one begins with its main concern of "devouring wealth ... falsely," which fundamentally means to take wealth from another without giving something of value in return. It then proceeds with the threat of hell against those who "hoard up gold and silver and do not spend it in the way of God," as if to imply that currency should remain in circulation rather than withheld from the market. There is no other way to ensure the free exchange of goods and trade built on mutual goodwill. The verse also suggests that the rich are not to monopolize all the wealth. They should, rather, grant the poor access to it as well.

Although this verse was revealed during the Meccan period before there was a religious duty to pay *zakat* (obligatory tithe), multiple hadith specialists relate[10] that the second caliph of Islam, 'Umar b. al-Khattab, on one occasion questioned the Prophet Muhammad for clarity after hearing him curse gold and silver in relation to what is written in the Qur'an 9:34–35. 'Umar expressed the uneasiness felt by the Prophet's companions in light of the misapprehension that they were no longer allowed to possess and leave behind gold and silver to their offspring. Accordingly, the Prophet responded, "God imposed Zakat upon you only so that the remainder of your wealth will be deemed wholesome. And, He imposed inheritance upon wealth that remains after you leave [this world]" (Abu Dawud, hadith no. 1664).[11]

---

[10] The report is issued by Abu Dawud, Ibn Mardawayh, and Al-Hakim, who affirmed that the hadith fulfills Bukhari and Muslim's criteria of authenticity.

[11] Abu Dawud Sulayman b. al-Ash'ath Al-Sijistani, *Sunan Abu Dawud* [in Arabic], 7 vols., ed. S. Arnaut, M. K. Balali, and S. M. Al-Shayyab (Damascus, Syria: Dar al-Risalah al-'Alamiyyah, 2009), 3:97 (author's translation). Persian scholar Abu Dawud (d. AH 275/AD 889) collected the hadith (sayings of Prophet Muhammad) included in *Sunan Abu Dawud*, which is widely considered one of six canonical collections of hadith (Kutub as-Sittah). For an online and multilingual database

It is also said that this verse directly addresses the three chief influencers in society (*ru'us al-nas*), whose corruption leads to the collapse of civilization—that is, scholars, ascetics, and the wealthy. Ibn Kathir says,

> So, when the state of these is corrupted, thus follows the state of all people. As someone once said, "Is faith (*din*) not spoiled by anyone but kings, amoral scholars, and their monks?" where "kings" is a reference to "the wealthy" in light of the norm of kingly affluence and the etymological tie between the words "king" (*mulk*) and "property" (*milk*).[12]

That certain Muslim economists have accepted the belief that an Islamic currency does exist (in this case being gold and silver), this understanding may seem to be corroborated by the prohibition of hoarding the two precious metals in Qur'an 9:34–35. Some verses in the Qur'an also mention the "dinar" (3:75) and "dirham" (12:20), the prevalent currencies of the early Islamicate and surrounding empires. That notwithstanding, this conclusion appears to be merely implied and highly speculative, especially because dinars and dirhams were also in wide circulation in both the Persian and Byzantine Empires, some claiming that the very words originate from Persian, which itself is indicative of their non-Islamic origin. In addition, it is settled history that Muslims did not mint their own unique currency until the reign of the Umayyad caliph 'Abd Al-Malik b. Marwan (d. AH 86/AD 705). This means that before this, Muslims regularly transacted with currency bearing the distinct religious markings of the Christians and Zoroastrians, as proven by the

---

(English/Arabic with some also in Urdu) of these collections of hadith, plus more information about their collectors, see Sunnah.com at https://sunnah.com/.

[12] Ibn Kathir, *Tafsir al-Qur'an al-'Azim*. Beirut: Mu'assassah al-Kutub al-Thaqafiyyah, 1996, 2/335.

latest research.[13] This would mean that instead of dinars and dirhams being distinctly Islamic or Shariah-compliant currency, the very existence and prevalence of the two coins was merely coincidental to Arab and Muslim proximity to the two great empires of Persia and Byzantium. Furthermore, Imam Malik b. Anas (d. AH 179/AD 795) stated that even if Muslims were to begin to transact in hides, the rules for *riba* (usury) would still apply.[14] This means that in the view of Imam Malik, gold and silver were not necessarily Islamic currencies any more than they were convenient or universally valued media of exchange.

The very fact that Muslim economists and other thinkers reacting to Western civilizational hegemony fail to see political economies, government structures, and trade options as merely aspects of organic human evolutionary interaction and intercultural exchange reinforces notions and fuels anxieties related to the "clash of civilizations" narrative. The Prophet did not leave any clear direction on how to set up a government beyond emphasizing the importance of consultation, appointing those most fit for office, and denying office to those who ask for it as well as the obligation of justice and obedience to the ruler when those conditions exist as long as he is not ordering anyone to disobey God. He gave no specific direction on how to write a constitution, the branches of government, or term limits. There is also no definitive proof that he obligated Muslims

---

[13] For more on non-Arab contributions to early Arab-ruled Muslim societies, see the works of Professors Fred Donner, Richard Bulliet, and John Brockupp.

[14] Imam Malik said, "If hides were to become a common basis of exchange between people in the way that it happens with minted cash ('ayn maskūka), we would disapprove of its sale against gold and silver with delayed payment (i.e. equating it with a usurious transaction)." Quoted in Muḥammad al-Ta'wīl, "Zakat on Cash and Its Latest Developments: Why Silver Should Be the Basis for Appraising Zakat on Paper Money," trans. Abdullah bin Ḥamīd' 'Alī (Lamppost Education Initiative, 2011), https://lamppostedu.org/wp-content/uploads/2018/06/Zakat-on-Paper-Money.pdf.

to call their heads of state "caliphs" and their governmental structure a "caliphate." Rather, there is greater evidence that such titles simply mirror their political counterparts in other nations, like the shah (Persia), caesar (Roman Empire), pharaoh (Egypt), negus (Abyssinia), and tubba' (Yemen). Similar things can be said in the areas of economics and finance. There is little reason to believe the Prophet's intent was to construct an entirely new alternative economic system to what prevailed during his time.

Is it at all possible that there is actually neither an Islamic currency nor Islamic financing but merely currency and finance? Instead of Islam being viewed as the nemesis of the West and vice versa, is it not possible to simply embrace the assertion that intercultural exchange is a ubiquitous and transhistorical part of human interaction? The very Qur'an that Muslims read contains words from Arabic as well as words that originate from Hebrew, Persian, Syriac, Greek, and Abyssinian. Early Muslim rulers also adopted certain administrative norms of their imperial predecessors, employed Jews and other non-Muslims to important offices, and even allowed for censuses to be recorded in non-Arabic languages. That's not to mention that the Prophet Muhammad did not seem averse to cultural appropriation anytime he saw that some benefit would come to his followers and the Islamicate.

Although Islam obligates the *zakat* poor-due, there is little reason to believe that the religion favors a highly regulated market. For instance, the Prophet said, "The two parties of a sale have an option [to cancel] as long as they do not split company. So, if they are truthful and forthcoming, they will be blessed in their exchange. But, if they conceal [any defects] and lie, the blessing of their exchange is obliterated" (Al-Bukhari, hadith no. 2110).[15] He also said, "Let no resident [*hadir*] sell

---

[15] Muhammad b. Isma'il Al-Bukhari, *Sahih al-Bukhari* (Beirut: Dar Ibn Kathir, 2002), 508. Persian scholar Al-Bukhari (d. AH 256/AD 870) collected the hadith (sayings of Prophet Muhammad) included

for an outsider [*bad*]. Leave the people, and God will provide for some through others" (Al-Nisaburi, hadith no. 1522).[16]

The first hadith establishes a market rule concerning when deals are considered binding. This is so that while it also highlights the freedom of traders to set their own standards and prices, promising that as long as one does not aim to defraud the other, God will bless the exchange. And when God blesses an exchange, it contributes to the well-being of society since trust, the pillar of all healthy relationships, is promoted. The second hadith is even clearer regarding the importance of people being allowed to trade at a fair price agreed on between the two parties without the interference of outsiders who may believe they know better the interests of those in the more disadvantageous position.

The disadvantaged, according to contemporary anticapitalist ideology, is almost always the buyer since the wealthy are given default oppressor status. This status applies even if the buyer is content with making the purchase by his or her own free will. Consider this in the context of the debates concerning minimum wage, the living wage, the rights of foreign domestic workers, and undocumented immigrants from countries like Mexico. How often do we actually hear from the presumed exploited parties in such deals? Are they actually satisfied with the salaries they receive for their work? Or do we assume too much based on our own subjective standards of what is just and equitable?

Of course this is not to suggest that one should not be concerned with corporations that receive tax incentives in some

---

in *Sahih al-Bukhari*, which is widely considered one of six canonical collections of hadith (Kutub as-Sittah).

[16] Muslim b. al-Hajjaj Al-Nisaburi, *Sahih Muslim* (Riyadh: Dar Taybah, 2006), 709. Persian scholar Al-Nisaburi (d. AH 261/AD 875) collected the hadith (sayings of Prophet Muhammad) included in *Sahih Muslim*, which is widely considered one of six canonical collections of hadith (Kutub as-Sittah).

countries to employ that country's citizens, who then exploit loopholes in immigration laws in search of cheap labor elsewhere. Nor should we ignore the negative impact immigration policies can have on legal citizens who are among the least educated and lowest income earners. That's not to mention the importance of addressing the exploitation of child labor and the employment of impoverished people in sweatshops void of labor rights and protections. Despite all that has been mentioned, it is difficult to entertain doubt about the Prophet's own thoughts on regulatory norms after reading the following:

> The people said: "O Messenger of Allah! The prices are exorbitant. So regulate the prices for us." So the Mes-senger of Allah [PBUH[17]] said: "Verily Allah is the price regulator, The Constrictor [Al-Qabid], The Expander [Al-Basit],and The Provider [Al-Raziq]. And verily I hope to meet Allah while none of you demands from me the removal of an injustice [mazlima] in blood or in wealth." (Tirmidhi, hadith no. 1314)[18]

---

[17] Non-Muslim readers may find it helpful to know that the initialism "PBUH" in English-language writing represents an Arabic phrase that translates as "peace be upon him." Such benedictions on the Prophet Muhammad and major figures of the Islamic tradition are deemed by many Muslims to be a religious requirement. The reader will note various similar abbreviated benedictions that appear occasionally in this work and in quoted material—namely, "SAWS," meaning "God bless him and grant him peace" for the Prophet Muhammad; and "SWT," meaning "glorious and exalted is He" for Allah.

[18] Al-Tirmidhi, Abu 'Isa. Jami' al-Tirmidhi (Damascus & Riyadh: Dar al-Fayha & Dar al-Salam, 1999), 319. The hadith is reported by Tirmidhi (d. AH 279/AD 892), Abu Dawud (AH 275/AD 889), and Al-Nasa'i (AH 303/AD 915). They were all Persian scholars who collected the hadith (sayings of Prophet Muhammad) included respectively in Jami' al-Tirmidhi, Sunan Abi Dawud, and Sunan al-Nasa'i, which are widely considered among the six canonical collections of hadith (Kutub as-Sittah).

Notwithstanding, the religious duty to pay *zakat* and the moral imperative to provide for the poor and disadvantaged, the aforementioned Qur'anic verses, and prophetic traditions all point in the direction of support for free trade and free markets. This is despite the fact that the Prophet Muhammad audited market activities for fraud and assigned this task to others after him. But his idea of regulation seemed limited to keeping the market free of fraudulent practices while not usurping the ownership rights of any of those transacting in the market. His prohibition against market taxes further underscores this concern, saying in one tradition, "The one who charges a market tax [*sahib maks*] will not enter Paradise" (Abu Dawud, hadith no. 2937).[19]

ISLAM AS A RELIGIOUS ECONOMY

Perhaps what contributes to the apparent economic schizophrenia is the fact that Islam, like most premodern religions, does not clearly dislodge religion from politics or from economic well-being. Rather, Islam's character is an integrated tradition that only functionally separates between the ritualistic (*'ibadat*) and nonritualistic (*mu'amalat*), the sacred and secular realms. Unlike political economies, Islam's telos with the human person and human society is for both to become more virtuous. And that virtue cannot be realized if people are self-concerned and pursue only materialistic ends.

One could then argue that the main reason that "Islamic" alternatives to both capitalist and socialist theories are doomed to fail is that both of the latter two are squarely concerned with material outcomes and originate from a materialist view of the human being and his or her mission divorced from religion and spirituality. *Zakat*, for instance, cannot be viewed as a tax on the rich for the benefit of the poor—each defined subjectively

---

[19] Al-Sijistani, Abu Dawud Sulayman b. Ash'ath, *Sunan Abi Dawud* (Damascus: Dar al-Risalah al-'Alamiyyah, 2009), 4/526.

today—any more than it can be legitimately claimed that the objective of *zakat* is to eradicate poverty, thereby ushering in an economic utopia.

The first claim is not true because a Muslim is only obligated to pay *zakat* if he or she has an annual surplus after reaching a minimum payout threshold (*nisab*) that is maintained for an entire year. And a Muslim government is not allowed to simply extract 2.5 percent of a Muslim's annual income, poor or otherwise. Nor is it allowed to spend *zakat* income in any way the government deems fitting. Rather, the Qur'an designates eight categories of recipients for *zakat* (9:60). This is clearly not the way that taxes work in modern states. Furthermore, a Muslim is under no obligation to save his or her money after reaching the payout threshold. So it is permitted without condition for a person who would be obligated to pay *zakat* after a year's time to spend his or her savings prior to the twelfth-month deadline when the *zakat* payment becomes binding.

For these same reasons, it cannot be claimed that Islam aims to eradicate the world of poverty (even if it may aim to alleviate it), especially in light of the fact that the nature of this realm is change, not permanence. People move in and out of poverty and affluence sometimes due to the decisions they make. It would be wonderful for every person to own a house, but that is not likely to happen if someone is a spendthrift who wastes his or her earnings or refuses to work. Placing the responsibility of wealth in the hands of irresponsible people is more likely to lead them to either forfeit or destroy their property. It is for this very reason that Islam interdicts the transactions of minors, the insane, and the spendthrifts to prevent them from acting against their own interests. Additionally, the nature of the wealth subject to *zakat* (gold, silver, farm produce, and livestock) provides no guarantee that those to whom ownership of them is transferred will make the wisest use of the said valuables. They may just as likely sell one form of wealth for another that is far less valuable, lose or misplace it, or forfeit it in some other way. In a free market, such transfers would be the prerogative of all responsible adults. And only in such a market are possibilities maximized.

To claim that the raison d'être of *zakat* is the eradication of poverty is an unsupportable ratiocination. Accepting this assertion would lead to the abrogation of *zakat* once and for all under any given economic system that elevates every citizen beyond the standards of poverty. This would include a system that taxes the income of every person, including those who may have once been eligible recipients of *zakat* funds. Such a system would contravene the divine injunctions that tax only annual surplus, not income. It would ignore the spiritually "purifying" objective of *zakat* as related by the Qur'an: "Take from their wealth a charity which will purify them and help them to grow. And, pray for them" (9:103). It would be an authoritarian act reserved only for God. That's not to mention that one would also need to explain why the Qur'an designates a share of *zakat* to those who collect and distribute it as well as "those whose hearts are to be reconciled" to Islam (9:60). Neither group is presumptively among the impoverished classes. But once the putative objective of *zakat* is achieved, it follows logically that they would no longer be eligible to receive anything even though the Qur'an clearly grants them a right to share in *zakat*.

NONCOMPULSION POLICY

Qur'an 2:256 ("There is no compulsion in religion") is a verse oft recited by Muslims to underscore the argument that Islam does not allow for forced conversion. While considering the earlier assertion that the religious is also political and economic, one can extend this verse to mean that "there is no compulsion in political allegiance" and that "there is no compulsion in business transactions." Both assumptions were actually shared by Muslims since earliest times. When the Abbasid dynasty overthrew the incumbent Umayyads and tried to compel allegiance, many Muslim scholars and commoners resisted, objecting that such acts of coercion have no validity in Islam. Similarly, jurists, generally, ruled that anytime a person is compelled to sell property, the sale is legally invalid.

Of course all this has the potential to be undermined by the fact that Muslims and Islamic teachings, apparently, allow for compulsion of fellow Muslims in certain cases. Muhammad's first temporal successor, Abu Bakr, waged a war against many Muslims who refused to pay the *zakat* owed to the poor that the caliph was responsible for distributing. This, however, was viewed as an exception to the basic rule in light of the fealty oath that Muslims took with Muhammad before his demise. Muhammad's close companion 'Umar and others understood this oath to necessitate that fighting between Muslims was both unlawful and sinful. And 'Umar raised such a concern with Abu Bakr when he saw the latter poised to go to war. Abu Bakr insisted that his intention to confiscate *zakat* properties was due to him by the "right of Islam." Upon this, 'Umar's heart was reconciled to Abu Bakr's mission.

That notwithstanding, the Muhammadan ethos was characterized by a policy of gentle persuasion rather than compulsion. Since his primary concern was the eternal salvation of all human souls, this policy makes wise sense. There are so many examples of his employment of this ethic throughout his life. We have already seen his reluctance to fix prices in the market, saying, "I hope to meet Allah while none of you demands from me the removal of an injustice [*mazlima*] in blood or in wealth" (Tirmidhi, hadith no. 1314).[20] If one of them were to demand the removal of an injustice from the Prophet or even accuse him of being unjust, it would constitute a rejection of his message and mission that would ultimately result in the person's damnation. But Muhammad, seeking not to needlessly anger his followers, avoided such decisions to protect their hearts from

[20] Al-Tirmidhi, Abu 'Isa. Jami' al-Tirmidhi (Damascus & Riyadh: Dar al-Fayha & Dar al-Salam, 1999), 319. The hadith is reported by Tirmidhi (d. AH 279/AD 892), Abu Dawud (AH 275/AD 889), and Al-Nasa'i (AH 303/AD 915).

entertaining resentment toward him. He never hit a child, a servant, or a woman. He never made those serving him feel uneasy for failing to complete a task. When his wives annoyed him, he left the home, perhaps out of fear that divine chastisement would descend on them in his presence. And on more than one occasion, when Bedouins accused him of an unjust division of spoils, he bore the abuse patiently and continued to give to his detractors until they were content. All this highlights the degree of importance that Islam has placed on freedom of action and especially the freedom to trade as one pleases.

Under current socialistic demands, however, people would be compelled to share their wealth or have it stripped from them by force. The wealthy would be expected to continue to exert the same amount of effort for small percentages of their earnings while giving the larger profits to others who contributed nothing to them. There is no doubt that this would be a disincentive for business. And it would be a clear injustice. Charity comes from the heart, and it loses all its meaning once it is made compulsory. It is for similar reasons that a Muslim is not obligated to place his zakatable surplus in escrow before it is due one year after reaching the zakatable threshold. In the absence of a just government to whom *zakat* can be paid, a Muslim must pay it to those eligible. If one refuses to pay it, the sin is on him or her, and one's reckoning is with God.

CONCLUSION

One must not lose sight of the fact that Islam's greatest concerns are with the ultimate salvation of the human soul after death and societal harmony. The spiritual dimension of its teachings makes it difficult to reconcile as an alternative material solution to ethereal problems. Both capitalism and social-ism are too limited in scope and insufficient for helping people achieve happiness in this world. This is precisely because one's happiness is just as much tied to one's outlook and sense of gratitude as it is to one's economic well-being. Both economic theories appear to be materialist solutions for human emotional dissonance, as if to suggest that unhappiness in our lives can be reduced to the single factor of economic upheaval. Islam as a holistic and integrated tradition begs to differ. The Prophet Muhammad said, "If the son of Adam had two valleys of wealth, he would want a third. But, the only thing that will fill the interior of the son of Adam is soil" (Muslim, hadith no. 1050).[21] He also said, "Affluence means the richness of the soul" (Muslim, hadith no. 1051).[22] In other words, discontent plays a major part in our relative unhappiness. Material well-being alone cannot calm the flames of greed, lust, and injustice. That can happen only when morality, temperance, discipline, and gratitude for the blessings given to us by God play a greater role in our lives.

This is not to say that the potential correctives offered by either capitalism or socialism play no part at all in contributing to a better world. They actually do. But no amount of imbalance can be corrected with another extreme imbalance. This is fundamentally what I believe is being prescribed when capitalism is demonized as an inherently evil economic system whose merits are accessible only to economic elites. Rather, I would argue that the merits of a capitalistic system are overshadowed by exploitative and oppressive operatives who have profited at the expense of significant populations. This is what drives the push for alternative systems like socialism, or at least aspects of it considered attractive in light of the failings of regulators to excise the system of fraud. One must also consider the roles that rebellion against God, traditional values, and hyperconsumerism also play in our relative unhappiness. This is because oppression and exploitation are often two-way streets, with greed being the unifying principle on both Wall Street and Main Street. That is, we share culpability in our own unhap-

---

[21] Al-Nawwawi, Yahya b. Sharaf, *Sharh Sahih Muslim*, 4/1/118, Beirut: Dar al-Fikr, 1995.

[22] *Sharh Sahih Muslim*, 4/1/119.

piness. That some of us get the upper hand at times does not cancel out our own attempts to exploit.

Islam seeks a proper balance between material and spiritual pursuits or at least attempts to assuage resentment over economic disparity. Unlike the socialist endeavor, Islam is not averse to social hierarchy. Nor is there good reason for anyone to believe that one of its goals is to create an egalitarian order. There is just not much evidence of either. It pursues moderation in all things. It encourages feeding the poor while simultaneously discouraging begging and prescribing work. The Prophet said, "For one of you to take his rope to gather firewood on his back [to sell] would be better for him than to beg anyone who might give or refuse him" (Bukhari, hadith no. 1470).[23] He forbade usury while discouraging people from incurring debt. He was reluctant to set market prices while at the same time forbidding merchants from hoarding, saying, "The hoarder is accursed" (Ibn Majah, hadith no. 2153).[24] One of his main concerns was the promotion of trust. It is said to be the main reason he forbade usury, consuming the wealth of others falsely as well as the sale of goods that are undeliver-able, undefined, and nonexistent. For whatever merits and promise people may see in socialist policies born of capitalistic failures, it seems clear that the Prophet Muhammad promoted private property—its protection, free enterprise, and free markets alongside regulatory procedures for circumventing fraud and the sale of harmful and unlawful goods.

---

[23] Al-Bukhari, Muhammad b. Isma'il, *Sahih al-Bukhari* (Damascus and Beirut: Dar Ibn Kathir, 2002), 358.

[24] Al-Qazwini, Muhammad b. Yazid, *Sunan Ibn Majah* (Cairo: Matba'ah Dar Ihya' al-Kutub al-'Arabiyyah, M.F.A. Al-Baqi edition), 1/278. Persian scholar Ibn Majah (d. AH 273/AD 887) collected the hadith (sayings of Prophet Muhammad) included in *Sunan Ibn Majah*, which is widely considered one of six canonical collections of hadith (Kutub as-Sittah).

ISLAM AND ECONOMICS

The current work by Ali Salman, *Islam and Economics*, is an extremely important and long overdue addition to the conversation about Islam and its contributions to economic justice. It challenges certain popular assumptions about the twentieth-century discipline of Islamic economics and presents an alternative framework for understanding Qur'anic and extra-Qur'anic economic principles. Atypically, Salman advances a more balanced view of Islamic economic principles independent of strong reliance on capitalist or socialist assumptions. In chapter four of this primer, "Islamic Economic Framework: Historical Romance or Practical Prescription?," Salman says,

> Muslims should note that the Prophet Muhammad (PBUH) was not a revolutionary who established a system from scratch but rather a social reformer. He did not invent any new commercial law or economic policy. Based on his divine guidance, however, he introduced measures that enabled a fair and just society to develop. He proscribed price control because from his own experience he knew that it was unfair to traders. When he introduced various options of use of land that had been conquered by the Muslims' army, he was creating choices for his community while also thinking for future generations. When he proscribed Muslims from taking others' property unlawfully, he reinforced an important principle of a fair society. When he forbade usury in lending, he was eliminating an instrument of economic exploitation of his time.

Of course, this primer, *Islam and Economics*, will not be considered the final word on the topic of Islamic economics. Those who have come to embrace normative teachings on Islamic economics are likely to challenge many of its assumptions. One may naturally ask: What makes your theory more Islamic than that of the predecessors and pioneers of this discipline? and,

Why should I dismiss what I have already been taught about this subject? Salman's response is likely to be, "Read my book. And then let us talk more about it."

As with any discipline formed through the process of inductive survey of scripture and law, ideas are likely to evolve and improve, while others will remain points that constitute the integrals of different schools of thought. Salman's work is not beyond reproach. It is, however, a courageous start on the path of recalibrating Muslim legal, ethical, and philosophical understanding of a topic the proper grasp of which can mean the difference between human flourishing and multigenerational suffering.

—Shaykh Abdullah bin Hamid Ali, PhD
Assistant Professor of Islamic Law and Prophetic Tradition
Zaytuna College

Acknowledgments

I am indebted to several individuals and organizations for encouraging me on this intellectual journey. In 2012, Olaf Kellerhoff of the Friedrich Naumann Foundation suggested that I work on researching and writing about price freedom versus price control in Islam, and the foundation later published my monograph on this topic. In 2013, the UK-based Institute of Economic Affairs published an abridged version of this monograph in the form of an article in *Economic Affairs*. I recall that in 2016, I had a similar discussion with Kris Mauren, the cofounder and executive director of the Acton Institute, in which he showed interest in commissioning a biography on the Prophet Muhammad as a merchant. My interest in this topic was renewed in Malaysia. In 2017, when I showed my work to Malaysian academic Syed Farid Alatas, he highly encouraged me to expand these ideas. In 2017, in his famous visit to Malaysia that led to his detention by the "religious police" and eventually the banning of his books due to his advocacy for religious freedom, Turkish journalist Mustafa Akyol showed interest in my work. It is an honor for me that he introduced me to the Acton Institute, which later commissioned this primer.

I am grateful for extensive editorial comments and guidance by Muhammad Khalid Masud, Benedikt Koehler, and Mustafa Akyol. I have also immensely benefited from Javed Ahmad Ghamidi, both from his books and in private discussions. I am grateful to Hassan Ilyas for pointing out some additional sources of relevant literature. I am also thankful to Dr. Janas Khan for finding me references for several hadith. I am extremely grateful to Imam Abdullah bin Hamid Ali for writing the foreword of this primer. I am deeply indebted to the copyeditor (who requested to remain anonymous) for his extensive editorial inputs, identifying several mistakes in references in my earlier draft and for pointing out more reliable sources. I am also grateful for all members of the focus-group discussion that the Acton Institute arranged for feedback and detailed commentary in 2019, including Mustafa Akyol, Syed Kamall, Ayman Reda, Rania Al-Bawwab, Nathan Mech, Kamran Bukhari, Admir Cavalic, Fida Ur Rahman, Edo Omercevic, and Rizwan Kadir. I should also acknowledge that my affiliation with Islam & Liberty Network (formerly Istanbul Network for Liberty) also provided an excuse for keeping in touch with the subject. My colleagues at the Institute for Democracy and Economic Affairs (IDEAS) Malaysia kept showing a deep interest in this work, which was a positive reinforcement.

Last, but not least, I am truly indebted to my wife, Shagufta, and our children, Ameer, Haider, and Muhammad, from whom I took away several weekends during 2018 and 2019. Without those weekends and early mornings, I would not have completed this work.

Despite all this enormous and most generous support I have received from friends, family, and colleagues, I assume responsibility for any errors that this primer may still contain. I pray to Allah to accept this work as "beneficial knowledge."

INTRODUCTION

In pre-Islamic Arabia, the city of Mecca, which hosted the cube-shaped Kaaba as the holy place for worship, was a melting pot of religion, commerce, and politics. Tribes from afar would travel to both pay their respects at the Kaaba and to engage in commerce. The custodians of the Kaaba, the tribe of Quraish, enjoyed peace and security in the midst of an otherwise tumultuous Arabia. Even the Qur'an would provide a divine testimony later for the accustomed security of their caravans in the winter and the summer. They were also accepted in their leadership role and never faced hindrance in their trade caravans. Thus, their religious role, as custodians of the holy land, granted them both political and commercial advantages.

Prophet Muhammad (PBUH) (d. AH 11/AD 632), who belonged to the tribe of Quraish, inherited a rich tradition of commerce. Before he claimed, at the age of forty, that the angel Gabriel had revealed God's message to him, he was well-known in Mecca and Arabia as *sadiq* and *amin*, or "truthful" and "trustworthy." He was an established man of commerce to whom people would come for resolution of disputes. This background would allow him to leave behind a rich heritage of insight, knowledge, and ethical principles about the economy.

This primer is an introductory text to rediscover these ethical principles and practical rules of commerce and economics, as revealed in the Qur'an, espoused by Hadith (narrations of Prophet Muhammad) and Sunnah (practices of Prophet Muhammad). The text also benefits from and develops critique on the contributions made by jurists and contemporary thinkers on Islamic economics.

As a religion, Islam offers three definitive and broad moral principles of the economic organization of a society that evolved in the initial phase of Islamic history. These are (1) the *principle of ownership*, which clearly delineates private and public property; (2) the *principle of wealth creation*, which is based on voluntary trade and price freedom; and (3) the *principle of wealth distribution* by circulation and assignment of rights. Based on these principles and using primary sources of Islamic knowledge, this primer derives a framework of operational institutional tenets that can be used to reform an economic system. These tenets are price freedom, free trade, market regulations, sound currency, *riba*-free banking, low and flat taxes, reliance on voluntary contributions, and strict inheritance distribution. Thus, the Islamic economic framework presented here in this work addresses all important business, policy, and equity issues that any economic system should resolve. In the present work, the Islamic economic framework, essentially built on a classical understanding of Islam, widens the discussion on the modern discipline of "Islamic economics"[1] and in some cases deviates from it, which has often been wrongly confined to banking and redistributive issues.[2]

---

[1] In this text, when I refer to the formal contemporary discipline, I use "Islamic economics" in quotation marks, and I use the term *Islamic Economic Framework* to refer to the view I have adopted. This distinction is important to differentiate the interpretations of Islamic principles on the economy.

[2] For a detailed critique of "Islamic economics" as a discipline, in which I draw similar conclusions, see appendix 1.

In fact, all religions, including Islam, have presented normative and ethical perspectives on economic matters. What make the Islamic case unique are the practical dimensions of these principles. We discover a comprehensive code of economic governance through Hadith and Sunnah of the Prophet Muhammad. Qur'an mentions that wealth grows through *sadaqah* (charity) and decreases due to *riba* (usury). Others have brought forth similar perspectives on Islam and economics. After reading both of Adam Smith's masterpieces, *Theory of Moral Sentiments* and *The Wealth of Nations*,[3] the authors of a textbook titled *Introduction to Islamic Economics* suggest that "original visions of Islam and Smith converge."[4] Moreover, they point out that "Islamic economics"—a collectivist reinterpretation of Islam's economic vision that emerged in the mid-twentieth century—is "diametrically opposed" to the conventional understanding of Islam's economic heritage.[5] They conclude that the "Islamic economic system is a market-based system, where markets are seen as the best and most efficient mechanism for resource allocation. But valuing markets for their efficiency is not the same as upholding markets as an ideology and a philosophy."[6] This helps elucidate the economic philosophy of Islam: it embraces a utilitarian dimension of markets but subjects markets to their own ethical framework.

[3] Adam Smith, *The Theory of Moral Sentiments, or, An Essay towards an Analysis of the Principles by Which Men Naturally Judge Concerning the Conduct and Character, First of Their Neighbors, and Afterwards of Themselves* (London: Printed for Andrew Millar, in the Strand; and Alexander Kincaid and J. Bell, in Edinburgh, 1759); Adam Smith, *An Inquiry into the Nature and Causes of the Wealth of Nations*, 2 vols. (London: W. Strahan and T. Cadell, 1776).

[4] Hossein Askari, Zamir Iqbal, and Abbas Mirakhor, *Introduction to Islamic Economics: Theory and Application*, Wiley Finance (Hoboken, NJ: Wiley & Sons, 2015), 7.

[5] Askari, Iqbal, and Mirakhor, *Introduction to Islamic Economics*, 7.

[6] Askari, Iqbal, and Mirakhor, *Introduction to Islamic Economics*, 27.

Even the eminent Pakistani Islamist Sayyid Abu-'Ala Mawdudi (d. 1979) affirmed the same idea when he said, "Human freedom is of prime importance to Islam, which builds the entire edifice of the community, growth and development on the cornerstone of this freedom."[7]

The Islamic economic framework should not be understood as a prelude to a new academic discipline or to a new economics, for that matter. This framework can be understood as a combination of moral principles and practical rules for a just, inclusive, and dynamic economic organization of society. At best, it can be understood as a doctrine, though without any claims of sacredness.

One can argue that a selective reading of religious texts can generate a doctrine that is consistent with one's own worldview. Thus, if I believe that open markets offer a better solution for uplifting the economic miseries of people than central planning, then I will only quote the religious texts that favor this view. Thus, religious case becomes a tool to claim legitimacy. If we do not overlook various aspects of a religious tradition, however, we should have the authority to offer interpretations of it by taking some of its parts as more pivotal. In fact, all human beings do this whenever they interpret and socialize a divine doctrine, but just because they do this does not mean that they should claim absolute authority. This humility enriches our understanding of religion itself, yet we must do this without ignoring other views.

One legitimate question is that even if we admit that the Islamic case for economic liberty is an authentic narrative, does it have any relevance for the modern challenges posed by economic organization at the global level? In a world where notions about income and wealth inequality are dominating every other debate, where does an Islamic conception of economic policy fit? Do Islamic foundations of economic liberty

---

[7] Mawdudi, Sayyid Abu-'Ala, *First Principles of Islamic Economics* (Leister: Islamic Foundation, 2011), 91.

offer any unique insights with a functional relevance, or do they present only moral injunctions? This treatise claims that the Islamic principles of economic organization go beyond moral instructions and do have operational relevance. It also posits that the ethical boundaries that Islam defines can be used as a guideline by which voluntary cooperation may not suffice. Of course this is a matter of belief, but these practical instructions can be considered by all, irrespective of belief.

This treatise is arranged in two sections. The first section provides the principles of economics in Islam—that is, the foundations of the Islamic economic framework being presented in this work, in which the concepts of private ownership, utilization of land and natural resources, and wealth creation and circulation are introduced. The second section develops an institutional framework, discussing key institutions such as price freedom, market regulation, fiscal policy, social protection, and provision of credit. The primer concludes with thoughts on the applicability of these principles and institutions today. The appendices provide an overview of the evolution of economic thought in Islam with a critical review of modern-day "Islamic economics." This discussion provides examples of evolution of thought in leading clerics and scholars of the modern age.

1

ISLAM, MARKETS, MORALITY, AND JUSTICE

L et us unpack these heavily loaded terms: *Islam, markets, morality,* and *justice.* Islam is an Abrahamic, monotheistic religion whose followers are known as Muslims. Literally, the term *Islam* means "peaceful submission." It is associated with the Prophet Muhammad on whom *al-Qur'ān* (hereafter, the Qur'an[1]) as the divine word was revealed. Historically speaking, Prophet Muhammad is not the founder of Islam, but rather called his compatriots to the same faith as pronounced and practiced by Abraham with some reforms. The essential feature of Islam, as he explained, was *tawhid*—monotheism in the name of which he challenged the idolatrous practices of Meccans. Before prophethood, which he received at the age of forty, Muhammad had spent several years as a successful merchant. He was also sometimes called to settle disputes among fellow tribesmen before his prophethood. As soon as he announced that he had started receiving God's words, however, he faced vio-

---

[1]As Qur'anic translator N. J. Dawood notes in his introduction, "The Arabic name (Qur'ān) means 'The Recital.'" N. J. Dawood, trans., *The Koran,* 5th rev. ed., Penguin Classics (London: Penguin Books, 1999), xviii. Unless otherwise noted, all quotations from the Qur'an are taken from this fifth revised edition of Dawood's translation.

lent opposition. Muhammad spent thirteen years preaching the faith and calling his compatriots to reform themselves before he decided, along with his companions, to migrate to another city, Medina. After migration, known as *hijra*, Muhammad built his community and eventually his rubric of a state with its own authority over the subjects. He lived for another ten years after *hijra*, during which he developed a basic framework for public administration comprising moral, legal, and procedural code along with religious and ritualistic codes for practicing Islam.

At the simplest level, Islam today means the word of God as revealed to Muhammad during these twenty-three years and known as the Qur'an as a divine text, along with his own sayings and deeds that he sanctioned during his lifetime. Throughout the last fourteen centuries, Islamic civilization has experienced a large number of human interpretations, starting with the companions of the Prophet Muhammad to contemporary scholars, rulers, and common Muslims. Given the complexity associated with a critical review of human interpretations and the rather limited scope of this primer, I will mainly focus on the primary sources of Islam—namely, Qur'an, Hadith, and Sunnah. The intention is not to offer any new interpretation but to present a snapshot of broad economic principles and institutions that emerges from a holistic study of the primary sources of Islam.

Market, in this primer, is meant to denote a social institution that comes into being with the interaction of at least two individuals for a single transaction with the expectation of at least some material gain. In the context of this discussion, a market is characterized by a voluntary exchange with mutual consent that is driven by certain rules either defined by the government or by the parties involved in a transaction. Market is more commonly known as a physical place, where one set of individuals would offer a set of goods and services to another set of individuals with demand of these goods and services at a price.

Morality, at a most simple level, is the idea of what is right and what is wrong. For instance, making moral choices involves making a distinction between truth and falsehood, between honesty and corruption, and between respect and disrespect. In the Qur'an, believers learn that God has given all human beings an innate ability to distinguish right from wrong (91:8). We also know it as conscientiousness. We learn morals through formal education from our parents and from our interactions with others. Also, we live under law and regulations that provide material rewards and punishments for certain types of behavior.

Justice is probably the most complex of these terms to conceptualize. For some, justice is liberty, and for others, justice is equality. *Liberty* itself has two meanings—positive liberty, which is the freedom to do something; and negative liberty, which is freedom from the coercion of others. *Equality*, at least in a materialistic sense, translates into equality in economic conditions. For some, this should be limited to equality in opportunities and not outcomes. Both conceptualizations lead to different policy prescriptions. American political philosopher John Rawls offered a principled reconciliation between liberty and equality and talked about justice as fairness.[2] His two principles of justice include the equal right of each person to a system of basic liberties and ensuring the greatest advantage to the least advantaged members of society. "Islamic economics" has primarily concerned itself with the theme of distributive justice. I take this Rawlsian view that justice has two conditions: equality before law and active support for disadvantaged members of society.

---

2 John Rawls, *A Theory of Justice* (Cambridge, MA: Belknap Press of Harvard University Press, 1971). See esp. chaps. 1 and 2, "Justice as Fairness" and "Two Principles of Justice."

2

PRINCIPLES OF THE ISLAMIC ECONOMIC FRAMEWORK

Islam offers broad and definitive principles for the economic organization of society that can be used as pillars for carving out economic policy as well as parameters for evaluating an economic system. These principles have a moral undertone with clear functional direction. We can find these principles elaborated in the Qur'an and in the traditions of Prophet Muhammad.

As we have noted, the Prophet Muhammad was an astute and successful merchant. It is not surprising that he provided essential incentives for his followers to create wealth. His model of wealth creation was a combination of private property rights and productive utilization of natural resources without owning them. *Zakat* was a low-rate, flat tax on income and wealth. The state deducted it from Muslims and distributed it to designated groups. There were no price controls, though strict limitations were imposed on certain types of commercial transactions and legal contracts to minimize the element of deception in business. This led to a business climate in which people were encouraged to do business in an honest, ethical manner.

In a recently published textbook on the subject of "Islamic economics," thus titled *Islamic Economics: Principles and Analysis* by the International Shari'ah Research Academy for Islamic

Finance Malaysia, to which almost all leading Islamic economists from the world have contributed,[1] we find the following concepts and operational principles. The concepts include *itqan* (efficiency), *adl* and *ihsan* (justice and generosity), and *ta'awun* (cooperation). The principles include competition, responsibility, and accountability.[2] While these operational principles are valid representations of Islamic ethos, they cannot be substituted for a complete system or framework. They represent, to some extent, elements of a moral order, which can be helpful to define an economic doctrine, but by themselves, they are insufficient to create a doctrine.

Javed Ahmad Ghamidi (b. 1951), a Pakistani Muslim theologian, includes five fundamental elements in his model of Islamic economy: private property rights, national control over natural assets, control over usurpation, documentation and evidence, and distribution of inheritance.[3] He argues that these five fundamentals of Islamic economy can be directly derived from the Qur'an. I find this list very helpful from a theological perspective and have attempted to explain these concepts in some of the chapters that follow.

I believe that any economic system should be able to answer these three fundamental questions: Who owns what? How is wealth created? And how should wealth be distributed? I base my own definition of a framework considering these questions.

---

[1] Adam Abdullah et al., *Islamic Economics: Principles and Analysis*, ed. Moutaz Abojeib, Mohamed Aslam Mohamed Haneef, and Mustafa Omar Mohammed (Kuala Lumpur, Malaysia: International Shari'ah Research Academy for Islamic Finance (ISRA)/Lorong University A, 2018).

[2] Abdullah et al., *Islamic Economics*, 145–47.

[3] Javed Ahmad Ghamidi, *Islam: A Comprehensive Introduction* [an English rendering of *Mizan*; citations in Arabic], trans. Shehzad Saleem (Lahore, Pakistan: Al-Mawrid, 2010), 465–66.

2.1. PRINCIPLE OF OWNERSHIP

The question of who owns what is central to economic policy. In a society in which the state owns everything, there is no incentive for individuals to create wealth because the wealth will not belong to them. Similarly, if everything is private property, then there will be no role in a society for a government to define a public order. Islamic traditions and jurisprudence have considered two main types of property: publicly owned and privately owned. They further have classified publicly owned property as state owned and community owned. These conceptualizations of property provide useful policy options and largely remain relevant today.

2.1.1. Public Ownership of Natural Resources

One of the most frequently recurring themes in Islamic discourse on economics is the ownership of natural resources, which are considered primary resources for wealth creation. We understand now that wealth creation cannot be confined just to natural resources. To a large degree, however, the physical development and infrastructure growth in a society even today is a function of exploiting and using natural resources. The debate about world economic order, international disputes, and geopolitics is still largely about oil and its substitutes, other fossil fuels, and increasingly about water—all naturally occurring substances on the planet. An equally important debate concerns the future of the Earth given the practices of exploitation and human consumption of these natural resources.

According to an academic work on the subject of "Islamic economics" titled *Economic Justice in Islam,* by professor of Arabic S. M. Yusuf (b. 1916), the most essential aspect of any economic system is wealth, its creation and distribution.[4] Yusuf further holds that the natural resources available to humankind are

---

[4] S. M. Yusuf, *Economic Justice in Islam* (New Delhi: Kitab Bhavan, 1988), 5.

central to wealth creation. He believes that Islam considers nature as largely a freely available resource to all without any proprietary rights to any individual. In fact, when it comes to nature and its manifestations, there is almost a consensus among Muslim scholars on the matter of ownership. Islam considers nature and natural resources as divinely owned and freely available to humankind. This is mentioned in several passages in the Qur'an, but the following verses capture it clearly:

> It was God who created the heavens and the earth. He has sent down water from the sky with which He brings forth fruits for your sustenance. He has subdued the ships which by His leave sail the ocean in your service. He has subdued the rivers for your benefit, and subdued for you the sun and the moon, which steadfastly pursue their courses. And He has subdued for you the night and the day. (14:32–34)

All jurists would likewise agree with Yusuf that natural resources are freely available to all humankind. They draw inspiration from a hadith that declares:

> Muslims have common share in three (things): grass, water and fire. (Sunan Abi Dawud, Book of Wages, hadith no. 3477)[5]

Drawing from above, Maulana Mawdudi writes that every gift of nature (air, light, heat, water, minerals, plants) is public and free unless it is private property.[6]

Yusuf further clarifies: "All the natural deposits—those which lie on the surface and those which are extracted from under-

---

[5] In most of the cases, citations to hadith quoted in this work have been taken from the website www.Sunnah.com, which is a comprehensive and authentic online collection of major works in *hadith.*

[6] Maulana Mawdudi, *First Principles of Islamic Economics* (Leicester: Islamic Foundation, 2011), 83.

ground—are categorized as public property."[7] But there is also disagreement: eminent jurist and scholar of our times, Mohammad Hashim Kamali (b. 1944) argues that according to *fiqh*, mineral resources that are found in private property belong to the owner of the land.[8]

There is also an interesting incident in the hadith literature that sheds some light on the dynamics of ownership of natural resources:

> Abyad went to the Messenger of Allah (ﷺ) and asked him for assigning him (the mines of) salt as fief. (The narrator Ibn al-Mutawakkil said: which was in Ma'arib.)
>
> So he assigned it to him as a fief. When he returned, a man in the meeting asked: "Do you know what you have assigned him as a fief? You have assigned him the perennial spring water. So he [the Prophet] took it back from him." (Abu Dawood, Kitab Al-Khiraj, hadith no. 3064)

This hadith establishes two points: first, it is permissible to allow private ownership for some natural resources; and second, "commons" (as earlier described including water, grass, and fire) cannot be given under private property.

The Qur'an mentions the word *ard* (earth or land) 458 times, but, as noted by Islamic economist S. M. Hasan-uz-Zaman (b. 1932), not explicitly in terms of private ownership.[9] In fact, sometimes it refers to the land of paradise, other times to the land of Mecca, and still other times to various other places. After his extensive review of related Qur'anic passages, Hasan-uz-Zaman

---

[7] Yusuf, *Economic Justice in Islam*, 30.

[8] Mohammad Hashim Kamali, *Maqāṣid Al-Sharī'ah Made Simple*, Occasional Papers Series 13 (London: International Institute of Islamic Thought, 2008), https://doi.org/10.2307/j.ctvkc67vz.

[9] S. M. Hasan-uz-Zaman, *Economic Functions of an Islamic State (The Early Experience)*, rev. ed., Islamic Economic Series 14 (Karachi, Pakistan: Islamic Foundation, 1991), 31.

concludes that "while [it] proves the lack of Qur'anic approval of private ownership of natural resources, it equally proves the absence of Qur'anic disapproval."[10] This conclusion, however, seems to follow an assumption that natural resources (e.g., *ard*) and wealth (*mal*) are one and the same. But this assumption is flawed because a naturally occurring substance such as a mineral does not automatically become useful unless human effort is invested in mining, processing, and refining it. Once human effort is invested, then that natural resource can become wealth.

From the preceding discussion, it may seem that Islam has declared wealth as private property but the earth itself as divine property. The practice of the Prophet Muhammad establishes that the leadership of the Muslim community, and subsequently the state, is the custodian of the divine ownership of the earth and its natural resources. The following hadith seems to define this principle clearly:

> The land is the land of Allah, and the servants are the servants of Allah. If anyone brings barren land into cultivation, he has more right to it. (Sunan Abi Dawood, hadith no. 3076)[11]

The above hadith simultaneously acknowledges both Allah's absolute ownership of the land and human ownership of the land due to people's investment of effort. Human labor, in other words, legitimizes the transfer of ownership from God to human beings. This idea of human ownership of land involves certain implications that are noted in the following verse from the Qur'an:

> Know that one-fifth of your spoils shall belong to God, the Apostle, the Apostle's kinsfolk, the orphans, the desti-tute, and the traveler in need. (8:41)

---

[10] Hasan-uz-Zaman, *Economic Functions of an Islamic State*, 31.

[11] Sunan Abi Dawud, Book 20, hadith No. 3076, accessed March 22, 2020, https://sunnah.com/abudawud/20/149.

Ghamidi interprets this verse to evolve a general principle for policy: "Wealth and assets which are not in the ownership of an individual or cannot be in his ownership should remain in the ownership of the state so that besides fulfilling some other needs of the state through them they are directed to those sectors of the society which are dependent on others for their needs."[12]

Certain examples from the life of the Prophet Muhammad are also insightful. According to Ghamidi's *Mizan*, it is known that the Prophet Muhammad, in his times,

1. gave the lands of Khaybar for crop sharing,
2. left certain lands under the permanent control of certain people for whom these lands had been reserved,
3. regarded certain lands as *hima* (declared them reserved pastures),
4. left certain things to be shared equally by everyone, and
5. fixed the principle of *al-aqrab fa al-aqrab* (nearest to the next nearest) for using the water of certain springs and canals.[13]

In addition, the caliph 'Umar imposed a fixed amount of tribute (*kharaj*) on the state-owned lands of Syria and Iraq conquered in his times, according to the extent of their produce while leaving them in the hands of their previous owners.[14]

It is obvious from this description that we run the risk of reductionism or selection bias if any one of these prophetic practices is adopted as a legal maxim and others are ignored. The fact that the Prophet adopted at least five different methods to treat conquered lands shows that a suitable strategy may be adopted in the light of circumstances.

---

[12] Ghamidi, *Islam*, 466.
[13] Ghamidi, *Islam*, 470.
[14] Ghamidi, *Islam*, 470.

It should be stressed that while nature and its gifts are considered public and free, human efforts to extract benefits and then provision of these benefits cannot be considered free and public property. For example, water is free, but human effort to obtain it, process it if needed, package it, and distribute it entails significant labor and investment, and hence the end product cannot be considered free of cost. If we take this argument further, one can establish that the companies in the business of selling mineral or purified water should be allowed to charge for all costs incurred in this process except for the raw water itself. This may sound unrealistic and ironic; the truth, however, is that the cost attributable to the water itself in a bottle of mineral water is minimal. The price is usually determined by purification process, packaging, transportation, and management cost. This explanation can resolve the apparent tension between privatization of water services and the Prophet's commandment to ensure communal ownership of water.

Islamic jurisprudence, or *fiqh*, uses the term *iqta* to define the mechanism of lease by which the state leases out the land and such resources to individuals and companies for development. This system offers a workable arrangement for development of natural resources such as fossil fuels without handing them over to private ownership. The state can also award a long-term lease to competitive bidders and can receive a 20 percent royalty as was originally proposed by the Prophet Muhammad. This ensures long-term stability for businesses without diluting the importance of collective ownership of natural resources.

Having considered these examples, it is useful to recall the hadith declaring "water, fire and grass" as belonging to the common ownership of the community. Notice also that ownership is attributed to "the community," but that does not automatically mean "the state." As we understand from the modern discussion of environmental economics, and especially of the management of commons led by Nobel laureate economist Elinor

Ostrom,[15] a strong case of community ownership of commons, which is distinct from both private and state ownership, has been established. This is consistent with the Islamic case for communal ownership of natural assets.

2.1.2. Sanctity of Private Property

Shari'ah provides for rights to private property, both moveable and immovable, as long as it is acquired through lawful means. This ownership also includes the freedom to dispose of the property in any lawful way. Private property rights extend to categories such as dwellings, capital, plant and equipment, and livestock. As long as ownership is rightful and legitimate, it is absolute. Ownership of property and wealth is considered a sacred trust.

The Qur'an acknowledges the sanctity of private ownership explicitly and implicitly as the following verses indicate:

> Believers, do not consume your wealth among yourselves in vanity, but rather trade with it with mutual consent. (4:29)

In the next verse, God reminds believers that it is He who created animals, and thereby the ownership of them is given to humankind:

> Do they not see how, among the things Our hands have made, We have created for them the beasts of which they are masters. (36:71)

There are several hadiths that affirm the same message. One such hadith occurs in the Prophet Muhammad's last sermon to believers, in which he says,

> Your blood (lives), your properties, and your honour are as sacred to one another like the sanctity of this

---

[15] For more on Ostrom's work, see the Nobel Prize website at https://www.nobelprize.org/prizes/economic-sciences/2009/ostrom/facts/.

Day of yours, in this town of yours, in this month of yours. You shall meet your Lord and He will ask you about your deeds. (Sahih al-Bukhari, Kitab Al-Tawheed, hadith no. 7447)[16]

From this hadith we deduce that property is equated with ownership. Renowned jurist Mustafa al-Zarqa provides the following definition of ownership: "An exclusive assignment under the Shari'ah which enables only the owner to control or dispose of it, unless there is a legal impediment (such as being minor, insane) against it."[17]

Hashim Kamali believes that this definition encompasses objects, their use, and rights over them as part and parcel of ownership. Kamali argues that it is private ownership—in contrast with communal or collective ownership—that is the "principal and prototype of ownership in Shari'ah."[18]

Kamali argues that collective ownership can be over three types of properties. The first set includes properties for use by the community, such as public schools, roads, rivers, and hospitals, none of which can be individually owned. The second set includes barren land, forests, and easily exploitable mineral resources. The third set includes the lands acquired in conquered territories through war, although 'Umar bin al-Khattab (d. AH 23/AD 644) restored original ownership after imposing a tax (*kharaj*) on these properties.[19]

In the Qur'an, one notices phrases such as "his wealth" (2:264), "their wealth" (2:261–62), "property of others" (2:188),

---

[16] Sahih Al- Bukhari, accessed March 22, 2020, https://sunnah.com/bukhari/97/73.

[17] Quoted in Kamali, *The Right to Life, Security, Privacy and Ownership in Islam*, Kuala Lumpur: International Institute of Advanced Islamic Studies Malaysia; Petaling Jaya, Malaysia: Ilmiah Publishers, 2013, 259.

[18] Kamali, *The Right to Life, Security, Privacy and Ownership in Islam*, 265.

[19] Kamali, *The Right to Life, Security, Privacy and Ownership in Islam*, 267–68.

and "your wealth" (4:2). In its frequent encouragement of spending on the poor, Qur'an always acknowledges that this wealth is privately owned, referring especially to goods like livestock, capital, dwellings, and metals. This is endorsed in phrases such as "you may retain your principal" (2:279), "take alms of their wealth" (9:103), and "for the poor Emigrants who have been driven out of their homes and deprived of their belongings" (59:8).

The sanctity and security of private property was not merely a matter of abstract theory, however, since Islamic states based on the *shari'ah* have historically protected private property. The most visible demonstration of this security was the institution of *waqf*, "charitable foundation," which remained intact until the era of colonization. This institution was essentially a private property that was taken over by colonial powers but was eventually transferred to national states after independence. Subsequently, these independent national states restricted the functions of *waqf* to only religious teachings instead of broad-based social purposes. Through the course of these events, a private institution that played a fundamental role in the socioeconomic development of Muslim societies was thus nationalized.

Expropriation of private property by the state without compensation—in other words, nationalization—has received conditional and implicit support from eminent contemporary scholars such as Hashim Kamali and several other jurists. He cites two important precedents in early Islam. On one occasion, Prophet Muhammad turned a land area in Medina into a feeding ground for horses owned by the people. On another occasion, the second caliph, 'Umar, allocated two pastures for "horses of *jihad*," which were privately owned, while ignoring the protests of the owners. Hashim Kamali reports that contemporary jurists have termed these acts as nationalization in the contemporary sense.[20] In 1964, the Cairo-based Al-Azhar

---

[20] Kamali, *The Right to Life, Security, Privacy and Ownership in Islam*, 288–90.

Islamic Research Academy also justified nationalization to restore "social justice" and "economic balance" in society.[21] It is somewhat ironic to note that these interpretations explicitly acknowledge the sanctity of private property rights in Islam but use circumstances to justify government actions leading to expropriation.

In all such cases, endorsement of nationalization can be traced back to incidents reported above. But the distinction between natural resources (such as green pastures) and a factory (in which significant human effort is involved) is often overlooked. Therefore, the analogy of reclassifying certain land areas for public benefit or for government interests should not have been used to justify nationalization of private industries. Hashim Kamali's discussion in this context can be interpreted as a justification of expropriation, but he cites grounds such as unlawful acquisition in the first place, public harm, and exploitation of consumers.[22] While there cannot be any disagreement with the grounds for expropriation in those cases, giving the government discretion to take over private property is debatable. A better way to interpret these policies is in terms of the modern practice of zoning. When the Prophet converted a land area of the city into grazing pasture for horses, he essentially redefined zoning. This is analogous to the modern practices of urban design and management in which a certain property can be reclassified as agricultural, industrial, or commercial.

Thus, invoking the argument of collective use of natural resources to justify nationalization of industries seems farfetched. Any productive assets developed under private ownership, such as factories or commercial enterprises, cannot therefore be nationalized unless these assets were acquired and developed unlawfully. This modern trend of nationalization

---

[21] Quoted in Kamali, *The Right to Life, Security, Privacy and Ownership in Islam*, 288–90.

[22] Kamali, *The Right to Life, Security, Privacy and Ownership in Islam*, 288–90.

that swept the Muslim world in the twentieth century was in fact a clear violation of sanctity of private property rights that Islam guarantees.

A contested issue in the modern context is land banking—namely, the process of accumulating developed assets, typically in urban areas, with the intention of receiving capital gains or of building property on the land in the future. It seems logical from the prior discussion that Islam would discourage land banking, especially when it mimics hoarding and becomes a major reason for price escalation, which results from holding the land for some years instead of developing it. Consequently, allowing the state to repossess undeveloped land after a certain time or at least to impose a tax on it would seem legitimate. This goes against the conventional understanding of absolute private ownership of land, but it is consistent with an Islamic approach. Moreover, this can also address one of the fundamental factors in asset inequality and affordability of housing.

This discussion of ownership leads us to conclude that what underlies an Islamic theory of ownership is a dynamic classification system—a taxonomy. Under this taxonomy, we see that natural resources are publicly owned, though this does not automatically mean they are owned by the state. Rather, these resources can also be developed and used through governance systems based on community ownership. On the one hand, for development purposes, the authority can allot these natural resources for development to individuals (or companies, for that matter) under certain limitations and contractual obligations. On the other hand, the assets that are the result of human effort become private property and are thus protected. This includes agricultural land, capital, plants and equipment, buildings, intellectual property, financial assets, and moveable assets. At the same time, ownership of the land is not forever because the state has the right to take back land on a case by case basis. Thus, we can resolve the apparent tension between public ownership of land and natural resources, and private ownership of assets based on human effort and productivity.

The combination of these two types of properties, along with a continuous process of evaluation, provides the necessary conditions for creating wealth as a result of entrepreneurial effort.

2.2. PRINCIPLE OF WEALTH CREATION

As I noted before, Islam was born into a world of merchants. Urban Arabs were known to excel in trade, as they had little else to rely on for livelihood. Their trade caravans, in which Muhammad also participated extensively before his prophetic mission, went as far as China and India.

In his book *Early Islam and the Birth of Capitalism*, historian of early economic and commercial practices in Islamic history and former banker Benedikt Koehler (b. 1953) argues that Muhammad produced a rather elaborate business and economic framework mainly counting on his own experience as a merchant:

> Muhammad gave his community along with a new religion a framework for its economy. Muhammad's economic policy promoted entrepreneurial initiative, efficient distribution of resources, and wealth creation, a framework for creating wealth that lasted centuries.[23]

This prophetic vision is also reflected in the Qur'an, which promotes wealth creation in such verses as this:

> Believers, do not consume your wealth among yourselves in vanity, but rather trade with it by mutual consent. (4:29)

Here believers are exhorted to consume their wealth through trade and mutual consent, which are indeed complementary, as fair trade can happen only voluntarily. At the same time, Allah

---

[23] Koehler, *Early Islam and the Birth of Capitalism*. Lanham, MD: Lexington Books, 2014, 16.

the Almighty forbids believers from spending their wealth "in vanity." In other words, believers are discouraged from wasteful consumption and are advised to save and invest in mutual trade. If we look at the wealthiest people of today, we can see the wisdom behind such commandments. One example is Warren Buffet, who, according to *Forbes*, as of March 15, 2020, is the third-richest individual in the world, with a net worth of around $76 billion.[24] According to the website Giving Pledge, Buffet has announced giving 99 percent of his wealth to charity in his lifetime or at his death.[25]

This culture of savings affirmed in the Qur'an is the key to wealth enhancement, as we know from our general experience. It also entails a clear policy message: the fiscal and monetary policy of a country should be designed to encourage saving, investment, and trade rather than anchoring it on consumption.

In the classical period of Islam, trade was not the only vehicle for wealth creation. Once a state was formed, Muslims actively engaged in warfare and acquired wealth through military victories, initially in Arabia and later in Persian and Byzantine power centers. The wealth acquired through military conquest was mainly divided into moveable property, which was accounted as war booty, but there was also immovable property, the land. After extensive deliberations, Muslims imposed a land tax, which amounted to one-tenth of the produce, and they allowed the original owners to possess and harvest the land instead of taking possession of the land themselves. This land tax was a significant addition in the revenue for the emerging Islamic Empire. It is obvious, however, that in the modern world dominated by nation-states, this source of revenue is not an option anymore.

---

[24] "World's Billionaires List: The Richest in 2020," *Forbes*, accessed March 15, 2020, https://www.forbes.com/billionaires/#68438969251c.

[25] "Warren Buffett—The Giving Pledge," accessed March 15, 2020, https://givingpledge.org/Pledger.aspx?id=177.

Shari'ah takes an encouraging stance on affluence and wealth as it encourages the acquisition of wealth through lawful means on the one hand and imposes no quantitative limits on it on the other hand.[26]

A market price always contains a fair amount of profit margin for the seller, and this is an established tenet of commerce that higher risk entails higher profits. This fact makes legislation about determining any rates of profits subjective. On the one hand, an importer assumes great risk by importing goods from a distant location and is not certain about the durability of those goods once imported. He also makes assumptions about supply from competitors in the same period. Thus, he may declare a price that will bring him profit proportionate to the risk he has taken. On the other hand, a local retailer, buying from a wholesaler or the importer, buys small quantities and sells to his customers at lesser risk.

Prophet Muhammad did not define any upper quantitative limit on the profit; he did define a moral limit, however, in these words:

> Profit follows responsibility. (Sunan Abi Dawood, Book of Wages, hadith no. 3510)[27]

This is an interesting hadith, as it can be interpreted as a guideline for companies in the modern context of social responsibility that includes consideration of people and planet along with profit, which is commonly referred to as the triple bottom line.

The celebrated Islamic historian and polymath Ibn-e Khaldun (d. AH 808/AD 1406) had elaborated such natural mechanisms regarding profit in these words:

---

[26] Kamali, *The Right to Life, Security, Privacy and Ownership in Islam*, 245.

[27] Sunnah, accessed March 22, 2020, https://sunnah.com/abudawud /24.

> It should be known that commerce means the attempt to make a profit by increasing capital, through buying goods at a low price and selling them at a higher price … The accrued amount is called "profit." The attempt to make such a profit may be undertaken by storing goods and holding them until the market has fluctuated from low prices to high prices. This will bring a large profit. Or the merchant may transport his goods to another country where they are more in demand than in his own, where he bought them. This will bring a large profit. Therefore, a veteran merchant said to a person who wanted to find out the truth about commerce: "I shall give it you in two words: Buy cheap and sell dear. That is commerce for you."[28]

Ibn-e Khaldun has rationalized the profit earned on the basis of the efforts made by the seller. As a matter of fact, Ibn-e Khaldun also advocated a pro-merchant, free-trade system whereby the merchant rightfully travels and explores new markets to keep his profits coming.

Wealth creation in general has received scant attention from authors and contributors within the modern discipline of "Islamic economics"; it remains a crucial component of the Islamic economic framework we are considering, however. As the above discussion shows, the legal and social environment must be developed in a manner that removes or minimizes obstacles to wealth creation. That is why this framework does not accept price controls and allows only a low, flat type of taxation including low or minimal tariffs. As we will discuss later, the institutional tenets of the Islamic economic framework are evidently pro-wealth creation, which is in sheer contrast to

---

[28] Quoted in Chris Berg and Andrew Kemp, "Islam's Free Market Heritage," *Institute of Public Affairs Review* 59, no. 1 (2007): 12, https://ipa.org.au/wp-content/uploads/archive/59–1_Islam+FreeMarket.pdf.

the laws and values generally practiced in most of the Muslim-majority countries today.

2.3. PRINCIPLE OF WEALTH CIRCULATION

The most debated economic challenge today is the level of inequality—in particular, the gaps of both assets and incomes between the highest- and lowest-income households. The Islamic economic framework addresses inequality in three dimensions in terms we need to understand about wealth circulation. First, what is the divine scheme as far as economic inequality is concerned? Second, what is the broad principle of wealth distribution? And third, what are the available instruments for wealth distribution?

The Qur'an mentions that socioeconomic inequality is part of the divine scheme. These differences provide incentives for the have-nots to move up the economic ladder while instilling a spirit of constant movement in the society. One key verse that demonstrates this acceptance of inequality as a divine scheme is as follows:

> Is it they who apportion your Lord's blessings? It is We who deal out to them their livelihood in this world, exalting some in rank above others, so that the one may take the other into his service. Better is your Lord's mercy than all their hoarded treasures. (Qur'an 43:32)

At a more mundane level, the main rationale of this material inequality is interdependence. This is obviously not a blanket permission to allow the creation of vast inequalities in society. And as becomes clear from the following verse, the Qur'an discourages wealth concentration. In fact, the most important principle that Islam establishes for wealth distribution is wealth circulation. This is declared in the following verse:

> [The spoils] shall not become the property of the rich among you. (59:7)

The specific context of the instruction above was spoils from war, but this has been generally understood and used to emphasize wealth circulation. The circulation takes place through trade as well as through taxes, which in the case of the Islamic economic framework constitutes *zakat, ushr,* and a possible land value tax.

As long as wealth is being circulated, causes continuous socioeconomic mobility, and helps in fostering interdependence, the inequality per se should be considered acceptable. This acceptance of inequality, however, will likely be unacceptable within the current intellectual environment, so it needs further explanation. Would this Islamic economic framework or its attendant laws tolerate the huge gaps of wealth ownership that exist today? The answer lies in careful consideration of how inequality is initially caused. We can understand how inequality as a result of sheer talent (a professional athlete or media guru earning an extraordinary income) or sheer entrepreneurial effort or indeed as a combination of both would be acceptable in principle. But what happens if, in general, the quantitative difference between the income earned by the top percentile and that by the lowest percentile is insurmountable?

The Islamic spirit demands that leadership should persuade top earners to allocate more resources for social uplifting over and above their obligatory level of tax payment. This may require the kind of moral persuasion that follows in the footsteps of the *hijra*—the historical migration of Prophet Muhammad and his companions from Mecca to Medina. The Prophet established, through moral persuasion, a social structure in which the host community, which was rich and established, in their wealth accepted their poor Muslim brothers and in many cases voluntarily gave up half their wealth. Of course this should be taken in spirit rather than in letter and should never lead to any legally enforced wealth redistribution. At an institutional level, this approach of using moral persuasion should lead to a proactive, state-led effort to encourage wealthy individuals to set up trusts, or *waqf*, as we will later explore, by offering these top earners generous incentives.

Private ownership is held sacrosanct both by explicit commands of the Prophet Muhammad and by implicit instruction from the Qur'an. This ownership is not absolute, however. By declaring that in our wealth there is a share for others, Islam clearly establishes the importance of wealth distribution while reinforcing the sanctity of private ownership.

> The righteous ... shall [be] sharing their goods with the beggars and the deprived. (Qur'an 51:19)

There are essentially two types of limitations that Islam brings on the ownership and possession of wealth. The first limitation is imposed on a continuous basis through certain taxes mentioned earlier. Circulating and distributing wealth are accomplished in Islam by making *zakat* (obligatory annual payment due on assets owned by Muslims at 2.5 percent of net value) and *ushr* (obligatory payment on agriculture produce at 10 percent of produce) strict religious obligations and by encouraging voluntary spending through *sadaqah* (charity). The second limitation is offered by inheritance laws, which are made explicit through a strict distributional formula. The inheritance law of Islam ensures that the wealth of the deceased is distributed equitably. The general ownership of wealth is significantly diluted by this formula, as only one-third of one's inheritance can be distributed at will. Two-thirds is distributed to one's legal heirs, from the nears and dears of family members. The state cannot inherit anything from this wealth, and hence any kind of inheritance or death tax is out of bounds in Islam.

In a well-structured paper, Indonesian academic Hafas Furqani presents a set of Islamic principles of wealth distribution that are worth mentioning here. According to Furqani, the Qur'anic principles of wealth distribution include

> the principle of *kasb* (whereby individuals must put their effort to attain his livelihood and the effort is the basis for a just reward), *rizq* (Allah has allocated provision to individuals upon His discretion and hence inequality will exist in society as part of test in human life), *amānah*

(all wealth essentially belongs to Allah SWT and individuals hold it as a trust which requires responsibility and accountability), *huquq* (there are rights of others in personal wealth that should be delivered obligatorily and voluntarily), *infāq* (spending wealth in the way of Allah, *fi sabilillah,* which also means spending for personal and social wellbeing is the only options in Islamic concept of distribution), and *'adalah* (establishing justice in distribution at personal and social level is the aim of Islamic distribution). These principles set the foundations for distributive justice framework and direction of Islamic distribution scheme towards an establishment of a just and equitable society.[29]

It can be argued that by following the Islamic spirit of wealth circulation and distribution, the level of inequality will be reduced.

For the life hereafter, a hadith throws some light on the gaps between the rich and the poor. According to al-Tirmidhi,

> The poor will enter the Jannah five hundred years before the rich (Al-Tirmidhi, hadith no. 487).[30]

Moreover, of the eighty-nine occasions the words *wealth* or *wealthy* are mentioned in the Qur'an, most of the time they are used as reminders to believers that our wealth is a test for us. There should not be any doubt that the more wealth one accumulates, the greater the accountability. It is for this reason alone that the Prophet of Islam truly told us that the poor will enter the Garden five hundred years before the rich. For of course,

---

[29] Hafas Furqani, "Theory of Distributive Justice in Islamic Perspective: A Conceptual Exploration" (6th International Conference on Islam and Liberty: Building an Islamic Case for Open Markets, Islamabad, Pakistan, 2018), https://islamandlibertynetwork.org/blog/2018/12/30/hafas6/.

[30] Al-Tirmidhi, Book 1, hadith No. 487, accessed March 22, 2020, https://sunnah.com/riyadussaliheen/1/487.

only the rich will be asked about not only the sources of their wealth but also about its use. A poor person deserves little trial for using his resources for the right ends, while a rich person deserves greater trial by a just God. It should indeed be the case.

CONCLUSION

At the most basic level, Islam offers three broad principles for organizing the economic life of a society: the principle of ownership by classifying between public and private properties, the principle of wealth creation by encouraging voluntary trade through mutual consent and open-market pricing, and the principle of wealth circulation by ensuring distribution and assignment of rights to claimants and nonclaimants.

Without private property rights, there is no incentive for an individual to conduct commerce and to advance materially. An absolute ownership of private property, however, that disregards appropriate use of that property is constrained by Islam. The gifts of nature—"water, fire and grass"—are treated as commons, and absolute private ownership of them is denied, as these resources are commonly owned by generations. If a person uses these gifts of nature to produce something, however, such as building one's own house or developing natural resources, then this no longer remains property of commons, but the product or result of this human effort becomes private.

Wealth can be created and expanded only through mutual trade that follows from mutual consent in a process in which entrepreneurs and traders enjoy a high level of freedom. Finally, what we rightfully earn remains ours, but a small portion of that wealth we have created is assigned to others—both members of the family and of society, even if they do not claim any rights. Yet even such rights are further diluted upon death, as Islamic inheritance laws minimize one's discretionary powers by limiting and guiding the distribution and circulation of wealth.

3

INSTITUTIONAL TENETS OF THE ISLAMIC ECONOMIC FRAMEWORK

The institutional tenets of the Islamic economic framework as presented here comprise of essential institutions required to run an economy. The principles behind this framework are developed based on my understanding of Islamic precepts, with an emphasis on the functionality of these principles. In other words, this framework is not just ethical (theory) but rather is ethical-functional (theory and practice). As such, this economic framework comprises price freedom; free trade; market regulations; gold, fiat currency, and central banking; *riba* (usury) and its alternative; fiscal policy; *waqf* (social protection of people by people); and law of inheritance.

3.1. PRICE FREEDOM

Price functions as the information powerhouse of the market.[1] It conveys the value for specific transactions between buyers and sellers reached by mutual consent and voluntary exchange. If

---

[1] This section (3.1) is taken and adapted from some of my earlier work, originally published in a slightly different form in *State Intervention in Commodity Markets: Discord between Economic Freedom and Social Justice in Islam* (Islamabad, Pakistan: Economic Freedom Network Pakistan/

this information is distorted either by state influence or due to collusion of market participants, then buyers and sellers make wrong decisions. Subsequently, markets become imperfect. Historically, Islam has encouraged trade and enterprise, which cannot flourish if prices do not convey the value of goods. But how have Islamic jurists dealt with price and price control? This section revisits religious sources and the opinions of jurists and also discusses related issues of price stability, profiteering, price control, hoarding, and exemptions.

3.1.1. Tasʻir (Price Control)

The issue of *tasʻir* (price control by the state) has puzzled Islamic jurists for centuries. The Qurʼan is silent on this matter, and therefore we are left with the hadiths (traditions) of the Prophet Muhammad as a benchmark to understand religious notions concerning price control within the Islamic framework. According to a tradition of the Prophet, *tasʻir* is forbidden, as it is an injustice and as the prices are determined by God. There are various hadiths conveying this incident. One of them reads as follows:

> The people said: "Messenger of Allah, prices have shot up, so fix prices for us." Thereupon the Messenger of Allah (ﷺ) said: "Allah is the one Who fixes prices, Who withholds, gives lavishly and provides, and I hope that when I meet Allah, none of you will have any claim on me for an injustice regarding blood or property."[2] (Sunan Abi Dawud, hadith No. 3451)

Friedrich-Naumann-Stiftung für die Freiheit, 2012), 1–23. Reprinted by permission of the author and the publisher.

[2] Abi Dawud, Hadith No. 3451, accessed March 22, 2020, https://sunnah.com/abudawud/24.

This hadith is recorded in some other major hadith collections.[3] One of the earliest versions of "state fiqh" is Kitab al-Kharaj (Book of Revenue),[4] compiled by Qadi Abu Yusuf (d. AH 182/AD 798), a direct disciple of Imam Abu Hanifa, founder of the Hanafi school of jurisprudence who was later appointed as qadi ul-qudda (chief justice) by the caliph Haroon ur Rasheed. He mentions three different incidents in which the Prophet gives the same replies in different words. In all incidents, the Prophet refuses to fix a price.[5] This book was used by the caliph and subsequent rulers as a working guide for state functions and responsibilities. It may be inferred, based on this book which became the law of the land in the Islamic Empire, that any attempts to control prices would have received scorn from Muslims.

The above-quoted hadith is the only primary source of Islamic legislation over price control. The variety of interpretations of this hadith, however, has led to divergent legal opinions, though if the words of the hadith are taken at face value it can be argued that in principle, *shari'ah* is against price control. The divergence in interpretations is also based on the well-entrenched notions of justice and service, to which I will attend later.

One group of jurists led by Imam Abu Hanifa (d. 150 AH/767 AD) and Imam Malik (d. 179 AH/795 AD), although they prohibit rulers from fixing prices, is in favor of *tas'ir* for larger public welfare. This notion has been elaborated by Ibn-e Taimiyya (d. 728 AH/1328 AD), who has held *tas'ir* as not only permissible but also obligatory in special circumstances pertaining to

---

[3] Sunan ibn Majah, Book 12, Hadith 2285n (https://sunnah.com/urn/1265200); Bulugh al-Maram, Book 7, Hadith 812 (https://sunnah.com/bulugh/7/38).

[4] Yaʻqūb Ibrāhīm al-Anṣārī al-Kūfī Abū Yūsūf, *Kitāb al-Kharāj* [in Arabic] (ca. AH 132/AD 750; Damascus: n.p., 1732), https://www.wdl.org/en/item/11225/.

[5] Abu Yusuf, *Kitab-ul-Khiraj*, trans. Nejatullah Siddiqi (Lahore: Islamic Publications, 1966), 155.

famines and wars. The other group of jurists, represented by Imam Shafi'i (d. 204 AH/820 AD) and Imam Ibn-e Hanbal (d. 240 AH/855 AD), is against *tas'ir* ab initio since they view the private property of the trader as sacrosanct over and above anything else and equate *tas'ir* with violation of this fundamental principle. In a way, this latter group is in favor of the literal interpretation of the hadith mentioned above and understands the letter of the law to hold ground.

Hanafi views are articulated by Hanafi scholar Burhan al-Din al-Marghinani (d. AH 593/AD 1197) as follows:

> The Sultan has no right to fix prices for people. (Because the Prophet (SAWS) said Allah is the price-giver ... also because declaration of price is the right of the seller ... So the Imam should not interfere except in a condition where welfare of the people demands it.[6]

Thus, the Hanafi school opens the vast ground of public welfare in order to allow price control, which was later adopted as an obligation, though the companions of the Prophet Muhammad in Medina who were demanding price control from the Prophet were also advocating this version of public welfare. The Prophet's repeated refusal to intervene and fix the price and the jurists' attribution of injustice to price control demands more introspection on the issues of price control, justice, and welfare.

Unlike the Hanafi (and Maliki) position, which brings in welfare of the consumers to legitimize price control, the Shafi'i-Hanbali tradition takes a broader view by considering its implications for both sellers and buyers.

Imam Shamuddeen Ibn Qudamah al-Maqdidi (d. AH 620/ AD 1223), a Hanbali jurist, has argued against any kind of state intervention in the market. He writes,

---

[6] Quoted in Muhammad Lawal Ahmad Bashar, "Price Control in an Islamic Economy إسلامي اقتصاد في التسعير," *Journal of King Abdulaziz University: Islamic Economics* 9, no. 1 (1997): 30.

In a way, the control of price may give rise to price rise. The traders from outside will not bring their goods in a place where they would be forced to sell them at a price against their wish. The local traders would hide the goods instead of selling. People would have less than their need, so they would offer a higher price to obtain the goods. Both parties (sellers and buyers) would lose; the sellers because they were prevented from selling their goods, and the buyers because there were prevented from fulfilling their needs. So this act will be termed as forbidden.[7]

A comparison of the two schools of thought would yield interesting insights. The Hanafi school admits that *tas'ir* is against hadith, but it notes concern about the possible exploitation by the traders due to high prices. This is an interpretation, and the hadith did not mention this situation. Even if we accept this interpretation as legally valid, however, the Hanafi school does not show a rational belief in the freedom of supply and demand, as it justifies noninterference based on a religious command only. On the other hand, the Hanbali school believes that it is price control itself that will add to the miseries of both sellers and buyers and thus rationalizes the hadith. Ibn Qudamah had clearly understood two harmful effects of price control: emergence of black markets and unsatisfied needs of consumers. Thus, for this school, price control is an anti-welfare policy when the needs of both sellers and buyers are considered. This should stand in stark contrast to the Hanafi school, which justifies price control on the pretext of buyers' welfare alone. (One should note that the gap between Hanafis and Hanbalis here is partly caused by the latter's more literalist and strict interpretation of the basic texts, which, in other issues, may cause different—arguably less inspiring—results).

---

[7] Bashar, "Price Control in an Islamic Economy اقتصاد إسلامي التسعير في," 32.

But jurisprudential schools are not uniform. Ibn Taimiyah, the fourteenth-century Hanbali jurist who was also a supporter of price control for public welfare, has not only made a different interpretation of the above-quoted hadith but also quotes two other ones to support his argument. First, he believes that this hadith was specific to the situation of Medina at that time, as almost all foodstuff was imported, and imposing a price control on an imported item would have resulted in food shortage. He ignores, however, that even if the price control is applied to local sellers only, the effect of price control would be the same. The local sellers would demonstrate the same business conduct.

Another hadith that Ibn Taimiyah has quoted to argue that the Prophet himself fixed prices is worth consideration:

> This concerns a dispute between two persons—one having a tree on the other's land. The landowner found the trespassing on his land by the tree-owner to be nuisance and so took the matter to the Prophet. The Prophet ordered the tree-owner to sell the tree to the landowner and accept compensation, or just simply give it to him. The man did neither. So, the Prophet, allowed the landowner to cut it down and he made the landowner pay the price of the tree.[8]

Ibn Taimiyah argues that what the Prophet did in both these cases was pricing. But his interpretation is debatable. It is evident from both traditions that the Prophet only settled a dispute between two private parties and instructed them to settle at a fair price. He did not fix the price himself but left that to be settled between the disputed parties.

Ibn Taimiyah further says, "If pricing may be done in response to one person's need, it is more logical to do it for the common public's need for food, clothing and housing, as these public needs are of far greater importance than the need of one

---

[8] Bashar, "Price Control in an Islamic Economy اقتصاد إسلامي في التسعير," 32.

individual."[9] But his extension from facilitating a settlement between two private parties to establishing public policy is also debatable. It is relatively easy to get information and establish facts about two specific individuals who are in a conflict and thus arrive at a just solution. It is almost impossible, however, to calculate the factors involved in the case of indefinite individuals, and these unknown variables are what characterize the true nature of the market. Consequently, the impossibility of any person or authority being able to calculate private costs and benefits is one of the most important rationales for allowing the market to be free of price controls.

3.1.2. Caliph 'Umar on Price Control

A related issue to state intervention in prices arises when a trader deliberately becomes involved in underselling so that by keeping his price below the prevalent market price, he deliberately crowds out his competitors. Does *shari'ah* also offer guidelines in the case of a price floor? There is apparently no hadith on this matter; the jurisprudence on this issue, however, has been based on an action of the caliph 'Umar and its varying interpretations of this incident. In this case, it seems that more than legality, it is an issue of history.

Imam Malik quotes an incident and develops his opinion in favor of state intervention to determine a price floor. Imam Shafi'i refers to the same incident but adds more details. But what is interesting from my perspective is that the intellectual division across the Shafi'i- and Maliki schools, as observed in the price control debate above, is maintained. Imam Malik reports as follows:

---

[9] Quoted in Abdul Azim Islahi, *Economic Concepts of Ibn Taimīyah*, Islamic Economics Series 12 (Leicester, UK: Islamic Foundation, 1988), 97, https://archive.org/details/EconomicConceptsOfIbnTaymiyyah.

> [Caliph] Umar bin Khattab passed by Hatib b. Balta'ah who was selling dried grapes in the market. Umar told him either to raise the price or leave the market.[10]

But Imam Shafi'i adds to this story:

> After rethinking Umar went to Hatib's house and told him, "that whatever I told you was neither an expert's opinion nor a verdict. It was only a personal concern for welfare of people. So, you can sell it at whatever rate you like and wherever you like."[11]

Based on this, Imam Shafi'i concludes:

> Nobody other than the owner has the right to appropriate it [commodity] or part of it without the complete willingness of the owner except under the condition where it becomes obligatory for the owner to sell his goods. And this situation is not one of them.[12]

Imam Shafi'i's contention is based on specific conditions for when it becomes obligatory for the owner to sell his goods. These conditions will be discussed later, though under normal circumstances, such intervention is not warranted. Although Caliph 'Umar intervened for the welfare of other traders but later retracted his intervention, he clarified that his warning should not be considered a verdict but rather an opinion.

3.1.3. Price Control and Justice

Ibn Taimiyah argues in support of price-fixing by the government in times of emergencies like famine and in the case of market imperfections. In the case of emergencies, he argues

---

[10] Bashar, "Price Control in an Islamic Economy اقتصاد إسلامي في التسعير," 31.

[11] Ibid., 31.

[12] Ibid., 31.

that "it is for the authority to compel a person to sell his goods at a *fair price* when people are in the need of it. For example, when he has surplus food and people are faced with starvation, he will be forced to sell at a *just price*" (italics added).[13] By imperfections, he implies situations like hoarding, when sellers abstain from selling their goods except at a higher price than the normal one, and at the same time people need these goods, they will be required to sell them at a "price of equivalent."[14] It is notable that even in these situations, Ibn Taimiyah has cautioned against any excessive action other than forcing the seller to sell the goods. He has emphasized fairness and justice, which should be done to both sellers and consumers.

"Market" describes the practice of voluntary exchange, not a welfare institution. Price, on the other hand, signals a value that a buyer derives from the transaction and gives an indication of the underlying cost for the seller. Therefore, conditioning price with administration of justice in the sense of public welfare is not warranted except in the case of emergencies. At least this was not indicated or even implied in the hadith on *tas'ir*, which actually forewarns Muslims of the injustice done to sellers as a result of price control.

3.1.4. The Letter and the Spirit of the Law

From the foregoing analysis of price control, it can be established that Islamic jurisprudence is divided over the issue of justification, scope, and rationale of price control, although a consensus exists that in principle, price control is forbidden by *shari'ah*. As the comparison of various opinions over price control has shown, this division (each admittedly problematic in its own right) can be classified into two schools: Hanafi-Maliki and Hanbali-Shafi'i. The Hanafi-Maliki school tends to accept *tas'ir* as inherently un-Islamic, though justifies it on the basis of welfare. This school has also elaborated methods of price

---

[13] Quoted in Abdul Azim Islahi, *Economic Concepts of Ibn Taimīyah*, 98.
[14] Ibid., 99.

determination with mutual consultations among the state, sellers, and buyers. On the other hand, the Hanbali-Shafiʻi school sticks to the literal and contextual meaning of the hadith on *tasʻir* and warns of the dangers that price control entails for public welfare at large. This school sticks to the notion of the sanctity of private property rights, a largely undisputed concept in Islam, and believes that enforcing a price control amounts to a coercive parting of goods—one's property—and is therefore forbidden. For the former school, price control can ensure welfare, or at least welfare may warrant price control; for the latter school, price control deteriorates welfare. This sharp intellectual tension in medieval Islamic history seems to have been lost on the relatively modern scholars of the collectivist-leaning "Islamic economics" in the nineteenth and twentieth centuries, as we shall see.

As far as the letter of the law is concerned, deriving directly from hadiths, it can be established that Islam presupposes an environment of free trade with minimum state intervention as a legitimate, naturally occurring social state, unless contraindicators are demonstrated. In principle, economic freedom is guaranteed, and there is a strong rationale for believing that this includes economic freedom of both buyers and sellers, which historically constitutes the central pillar of Islam's economic philosophy.

That this freedom comes with certain conditions is also well entrenched in the concept of *shariʻah* itself. The natural question that arises here is: If this conclusion is accepted, then does Islam prefer economic freedom over social justice? What happens to the concepts of *afw* (waivers), *ihsan* (virtue), and *sulh* (peace)? How can a regime that is supposedly noninterventionist by design reconcile economic freedom with its obligations toward its citizens who are poor, left out, and marginalized?

Here is an answer to the questions above: the welfare that forms the central tenet of an Islamic vision comes not from price controls and wealth distributions but from liberty, enterprise, and charity. The Islamic vision ensures consumer protection from theft, fraud, or coercion through both legal means and moral bindings. Thus, the protective side of an Islamic vision of economy is essentially focused on ensuring no harm rather than provisions and redistribution—it is *negative* in nature rather than positive. If a state based on this vision could protect its citizens from coercion in any form and from anyone, it almost guarantees welfare without directly providing for it. The institutional practice of both prohibiting price control and ensuring consumer protection constitutes two of the most important elements of an Islamic market.

Thus, it may be argued that the letter of the *shari'ah* calls for economic freedom, but its attendant systems of free and fair competition and consumer protection provide a basis for social justice. Seen this way, Islam provides its followers a firm, moral foundation for economic transactions.

3.2. FREE TRADE

Trade, during both wars and peace, was critical to pre-Islamic Arabs. They were known for undertaking global trade caravans—the venture of exchanging precious metals that Arabia possessed for silk from China or spices from India.

In such a trade-oriented society, it is not a surprise that after migrating to Medina and establishing the mosque, the next institution the Prophet of Islam established was the marketplace. It wasn't the first marketplace in that city; in fact, four marketplaces existed already. He introduced unique features in his new marketplace, however. He required that trade be allowed to occur in that market freely, without any charges or fees imposed on market participants, and appointed supervisors to prevent any fraud. It was a market without tariffs but with ethical rules.

By instituting an essentially tax-free market, Muhammad took a competitive advantage over others, which helped in redirecting the trade to the new community of Muslims. In doing so, he was laying down fundamental characteristics of a market economy. The underlying motivation, as we will see, was justice, fairness, and moral conduct.

In an economy with no indirect taxes, Islam essentially will favor zero tariffs. When Muhammad established the institution of market in Medina, he abolished all tariffs. And once established, this tax-free zone was quickly established as a thriving marketplace for all trade caravans coming into the city.

Despite this market-friendly tradition, significant tariffs on trade were imposed in the Middle East under the Muslims' rule and were "onerous," as noted by Koehler, and sometimes "taxes doubled prices."[15]

The *Encyclopaedia of Islamic Economy* has compiled some key factors that, in accordance with Islamic law, lead to price hikes. These factors mostly pertain to the practices of Arab society at that time and have both ethical and legal dimensions. Accordingly, the imposition of *maks* (sales tax or import levies)[16] is forbidden; the interference of a third party in the negotiations between buyer and seller (with or without intention to buy) is forbidden; and a kind of preemptive brokerage to intercept incoming traders before they arrive at the market is also forbidden.[17] These practices were restrained or forbidden by the Prophet himself for their presumptive contribution toward price hikes. One can infer that direct price fixing was not practiced, though factors that led to price hikes were closely monitored and supervised. Factors that are a result of human agency, as opposed to natural factors such as a shortage of goods, were always given preference. In this way, the Prophet set a clear example: The state should not be oblivious to price movements,

---

[15] Koehler, *Early Islam and the Birth of Capitalism*, 177.

[16] The term *maks* has a broader meaning than simply "tax"; it implies taxing people beyond *shari'ah* authorized levies.

[17] Muhammad Moinuddin Khan and M. H. Syed, eds., *Business and Trade in Islam*, vol. 2 of *Encyclopaedia of Islamic Economy* (New Delhi, India: Pentagon Press, 2009), s.v., "Factors of Price Hike (Conduction of Business)."

but rather than controlling or fixing prices, it should monitor and supervise the factors that contribute to price hikes.

3.3. MARKET REGULATIONS

The Islamic traditions assume that prevalent market prices truly represent the cost for the seller and value for the buyer. This information, however, may be distorted by certain unethical and unlawful actions by market participants, as well as natural factors such as famines. Islamic jurisprudence (*fiqh*) has defined five sources of intentional price distortion: *ghabn* (intentionally overvaluing or undervaluing), *ghish* (cheating by exaggerating the product features or adulterating the product), *najsh* (bidding up the price by a third party in the presence of the buyer and seller without an intention to actually buy), *ihtikar* (hoarding), and *mawama* (fore-buying). These forms of market distortion were identified by the Prophet himself and are thus considered unlawful with consensus. Since they were practiced in the times of the Prophet, their practical meaning was well understood by the people of the age, and therefore the exact implications of prohibition in these cases were explained by the interpreters of hadith and jurists.

3.3.1. Dealing with Violators: The Office of Muhtasib

The early Islamic state saw the appointment of a muhtasib (officer), or the organization of *hisba* (market inspector), in the city markets, largely for the purpose of inspection and regulation. The first *muhtasib* in Islamic history was 'Umar bin al-Khattab (d. AH 23/AD 644), one of the most trusted companions of the Prophet Muhammad, who after Muhammad's death became the second caliph of Islam. Essentially, the Prophet delegated his own tasks of visiting the markets for the purpose of inspection and weight measurements to 'Umar. As established, however, price-fixing was out of scope for *muhtasib*. Later on, another noted Islamic scholar, Al-Mawardi (d. 450 AH/1058 AD), elaborated the duties of *muhtasib*. For him, "the market supervisor (*muhtasib*) is simply a coordinator of [the] market-place on the principles of 'enjoining the right and forbidding the wrong.'"[18] His functions pertaining to the economic realm included inspection of measures, quality of products, and the uprightness of the contracts in the market.[19] His other duties included dealing with "market rigidities such as *bay al-gharar* [speculative sales], *najsh* [fake buyer], price discrimination, monopolistic practices, collusion, dumping, hoarding of necessities and others."[20] A *muhtasib* was authorized to give advice, issue reprimand, obstruct by force, threaten, imprison, or even expel participants from the market. Unlike hoarding, for which punishment by imprisonment is also allowed, in the case of violation of *tas'ir* (price control), no clear verdict seems available. It may be clarified, however, that even for hoarders, the first action that *hisbah* would take against them was to force them to sell their goods at the prevalent market rates. If the trader was found guilty again, then an imprisonment option would be considered. In other words, this was a comprehensive framework for competition, consumer protection, and enforcement of contracts.

It appears, then, that the intervention of an Islamic state in the market has been justified, subject to proper investigation, in these cases:

1. *coercion*—if the exchange between the buyer and seller is involuntary;

---

[18] To translate *ma'ruf* and *munkar* as "right" and "wrong" makes it relative. The original sense of *ma'ruf* is *'urf*, "practice," or "norm." Muhammad Khalid Masud, personal communication with author, circa 2012.

[19] Muhammad Khalid Masud, personal communication with author, January 2012.

[20] Ahmad Oran, "An Islamic Socio-Economic Public Interest Theory of Market Regulation," *Review of Islamic Economics* 14, no. 1 (January 1, 2010): 134.

2. *cheating*—if the information about the features or defects of a product or its market price is deliberately withheld from the buyer;

3. *collusion*—if the sellers collaborate to artificially bid up the prices;

4. *war and famines* for the larger public welfare under emergency;

5. *exorbitant price hikes* amounting to doubling the normal market price; and

6. *hoarding* in the case of foodstuffs.

3.3.2. Trade Restrictions

The Prophet Muhammad was a successful merchant of his time before assuming the mantle of prophethood and role of a social reformer. Mecca depended on trade for sustenance and had therefore developed several techniques for trade expansion. Over time, especially after the Prophet took the reign of Medina, he introduced several reforms in how trade and eventually agriculture business were practiced. For our understanding, these may be considered as business practice reforms.

It has been reported that during the time of the Prophet, most food items were imported into Medina. Some of the town traders used to rush to the city border to receive the goods earlier than the local market, buy them up, and mark up the prices before releasing the goods locally.

The Prophet forbade this practice. According to a hadith,

> We used to go ahead to meet the caravan and used to buy foodstuff from them. The Prophet (ﷺ) forbade us to sell it till it was carried to the market. (Sahih al-Bukhari, hadith No. 2166)[21]

This hadith can be better understood if the historical context for establishing a public exchange or a defined market area in Medina is explained.

After the *hijra*, the Prophet had established a marketplace in the city of Medina in which all traders were directed to engage in business.[22] Trading outside this area was not permitted. The hadith mentioned above prohibited the practice of local traders from going to meet the incoming trade caravans outside the city limits. The traders had been receiving a double advantage from this practice: first, they could cheat the caravan by lying about the prevalent prices and demand in the city and then buy their goods at an artificially low price; and second, they could then sell the goods back to the city buyers at an inflated price. Thus, these traders distorted the price by withholding significant market information from the sellers and buyers. This also amounts to injustice to the incoming traders, who would not be able to know the prevalent prices of their products in the local market and would be deprived of their fair profit. This practice would invariably increase the price of commodities as well.

Thus, the Prophet showed a way to control prices by forbidding this practice of the city traders without directly controlling prices per se. The Prophet did not prohibit the institution of middleman or broker through this hadith, but rather he defined a specific context (outside the city limits) in which the role of

---

[21] Al Bukhari, Sahih al Bukhari, Book of Sales and Trade, hadith No. 2166, accessed March 22, 2020, https://sunnah.com/bukhari/34.

[22] Benedikt Koehler, "The Economist Mohammed Ibn Abdullah (570–632)," *Economic Affairs* 31, no. 1 (2011): 109–11.

agency was restricted (no trading outside the defined market area) and defined a well-regulated market.

The basic motivation behind trade restrictions that are found in *shari'ah* seems to be the desire to remove elements of deception, ensure predictability, and institute fairness in commercial transactions.

In his book *Mizan*, Ghamidi provides a useful list of twenty-one prohibitive forms of trade practices that the Prophet forbade in his own time, which is being reproduced verbatim:

1. Selling something before its possession is taken.

2. Selling grain bought in mounds before bringing it to the place where it is sold.

3. Selling and purchasing done by a city-dweller for a villager.

4. Increasing one's bid in an auction just for deception.

5. Bargaining when someone else is bargaining.

6. Selling crop when it is still in the spikes.

7. Selling the dates which are on a date-tree in exchange for plucked dates.

8. Selling the fruits of trees for many years [in advance].

9. Leaving an unspecified exception in a bargain. One of its forms, for example was that the seller would say: "I sell my grain to you, but I will take something out of it."

10. A deal in which a person, without thinking, just touches the other person's cloth and a deal is made in this manner.

11. A deal in which people throw something towards one another and, in this way, a bargain is made.

12. A deal in which people sell camels by saying: "Whatever offspring this camel gives birth to and when that offspring gets pregnant, whatever it gives birth to, then the [last] offspring is bought by me."

13. Selling fruits of a tree before their quality and characteristics become evident.

14. Selling spikes before they turn white and become safe from calamities.

15. Selling a commodity which is defective, except when the buyer is informed of its defects.

16. Holding the milk of camels and goats in their udders before selling it.

17. Intercepting tradesmen and buying their merchandise before they reach the markets.

18. Making a deal by giving money in advance such that a person obtains the item after it is ready except if this transaction is carried out for a fixed measure, a specified weight and a definite period of time.

19. Adopting methods of crop-sharing in which the profit of the landlord is fixed beforehand.

20. Adopting methods of crop-sharing in which the production of a particular area of land is regarded as the right of the landlord.

21. Selling jointly owned properties without giving the shareholders a chance to buy them except if the ownership divisions are determined and the paths are separated.[23]

One can notice that these regulations address largely two types of businesses: commerce and agriculture. The ultimate focus, however, is on exchange. These regulations certainly go beyond a generalized emphasis on being fair, just, and honest. In fact, they attain the value of legal bindings and become the basis of Islamic finance. Applying these established regulations is then more generalized, encompassing virtually every kind of commercial transaction in modern life.

---

[23] Ghamidi, *Islam*, 471–72.

We can evolve a general framework of regulations based on these specific twenty-one prohibitions. The emphasis here is to identify what is *not* permissible rather than to instruct what needs to be done; in form it is a *negative* order or directive.

These proscriptions were directed against business transactions that had any of the following faults: they were concluded outside a regulated market, took advantage of information asymmetry between sellers and buyers, or were passed on deception or fraud. Islamic law would also provide for annulment of transactions or contracts in which it can be proven that the rights of one party have been violated or an undue advantage has been given to one party.

Ghamidi writes:

> These are the various forms of sale and purchase and crop-sharing which the Prophet prohibited in his times. Since all the above mentioned directives are based on the underlying bases of deceit and damage, the directive of prohibition will stand dissolved in circumstances in which these bases no longer exist, just as if, as a result of evolution and development of civilizations, these bases emerge in some new economic activity, then that activity will also stand prohibited.[24]

Not every scholar would agree that these directives will stand dissolved if the circumstances change. As we have seen in the discussion over price control (*tas'ir*), there is a significant difference of interpretation among jurists on literally applying the Prophet's prohibition of price control, and some notable jurists have taken a position exactly opposite to the instruction of the Prophet, arguing that price controls can be enforced to ensure general welfare.

Based on these prohibited forms of trade, modern-day scholars of Islam have generally concluded that any transaction with an element of *gharar* (deception or deceptive uncertainty) will

---

[24] Ghamidi, *Islam*, 472.

be prohibited. Obviously, all business transactions, by their nature, are uncertain; therefore, this prohibition cannot be applied to uncertainty in principle. The key word, however, is "deception" and not "uncertainty." That is why Islamic finance generally accepts short selling of at least fungible items, a practice maintained by farmers. The prohibition applies to a sale in which the seller is unlikely to be able to deliver at the specified future time. These regulations didn't remove uncertainty of the outcome of commercial transactions—one may still incur loss—but made the process much more transparent, fair, and predictable.

3.3.3. Hoarding: A Special Case of Abuse of Dominant Position

In Islam, traders acting as hoarders are dealt with sternly. According to a hadith:

> No one withholds goods till their price rises but a sinner. (Sunan Abi Dawud, hadith No. 3447)[25]

A review of relevant hadith suggests that hoarding (*ihtikar*) has two essential characteristics: mostly it applies to food supply and then the seller stocks the goods instead of selling them until the price rises.

It can be argued that mere storage of commodities, even for the long term, would not qualify to be classified as *ihtikar*. The specific condition of the market and the relative market power of the trader in question would determine the legal sanction for the purported hoarder. As a matter of fact, as noted in the *Encyclopaedia of Islamic Economy*, some speculative behavior is condoned: "Not all hoarders are sinners... He stores goods in

---

[25] Abu Dawud, *Sunan Abi Dawud*, chapter on Business Transactions, accessed March 22, 2020, https://sunnah.com/abudawud/24.

period of plenty and sells them in times of shortage where there is comparatively high demand of them."[26]

The following tradition is attributed to the Caliph 'Umar:

> There is no hoarding in our market, and men who have excess gold in their hands should not buy up one of God's provisions which he has sent to our courtyard and then hoard it against us. Someone who brings imported goods through great fatigue to himself in the summer and winters, that person is the guest of Umar. Let him sell what God wills and keep what God will.[27]

The above tradition implies two messages: 'Umar did not accept the principle of freedom of trade as justification for hoarding in the case of gold, and yet he justified hoarding in the case of commodities imported by traders. The restriction on hoarding gold was probably due to its use as a medium of exchange, and any restrictions in the flow of this or other precious metals as currency would increase the hardship for common people.

As traders are deemed to be violating a law already by hoarding, therefore they will not be exempted from *tas'ir* (price control). *Fiqh*, however, does not address the case of storage by an importer. Rationally speaking, the importer would have imported huge quantities of foodstuffs in order to keep its average costs at a minimum. Not all that food would be bought by the market instantly. For that reason, coordination between importers for the expected demand of the market is unlikely, as such coordination is also illegal. Therefore, it becomes very difficult to classify storage by an importer as hoarding.

Once an act of hoarding is witnessed and the facts established, then appropriate legal action is warranted. Even in the

---

[26] Khan and Syed, *Encyclopaedia of Islamic Economy*, 2:79, s.v., "Hoarding Not Allowed (Traits of Business)."

[27] Quoted in Khan and Syed, *Encyclopaedia of Islamic Economy*, 2:80., s.v., "Hoarding Not Allowed (Traits of Business)."

case of hoarding, however, there is diversity of opinion over its remedy. One view is that the state can force hoarders to sell their goods, but the state still cannot force them to sell at a fixed price. Thus, in fact, *tas'ir* remains forbidden; the state merely forces hoarding merchants to sell their goods at market price. The other view allows the state to imprison the hoarder and control the prices.

Many believe that a strong state will not allow market participants to exploit consumers. Hoarding or abnormal price hikes, however, should not be understood just as a manifestation of market failure. As Ibn Qudamah realized, price control itself can be responsible for causing both hoarding and price hikes. If the state enforces an artificial price ceiling on traders wherein the true and natural costs of the product are responsible for price escalation, then traders are likely to resort to hoarding. Moreover, hoarding will lead to a shortage of supply, which will result in price hikes. Thus, price control itself can start a vicious cycle of price instability, and Islamic jurists have understood and analyzed this problem very clearly.

3.3.4. Method of Intervention in Pricing

I have argued that in principle, *shari'ah* is against any kind of price control. Does this mean that *shari'ah* offers a free ride to all traders of the bazaar and provides no room for authorities to intervene? The obvious answer is no, as certain conditions have been defined by *shari'ah* that justify state intervention in pricing. One such condition in which Islamic law will justify state intervention in commodity markets is in cases of cheating, coercion, or theft if established after due procedure. The other condition of state intervention is a public emergency, as in the case of a war, famine, or other natural disaster. The Islamic state may not intervene outright in the case of hoarding because the situation of hoarding and the resulting behavior of speculation are subject to further investigation. The state must, first of all, establish that an act of hoarding has a considerable influence on setting the price, which is only possible in the case of monopolistic or collusive conduct. Then the intervention may take the form of a forced sale of the hoarded goods, though that too is to be per the prevalent market price. The last resort against the hoarder is civil imprisonment, which may be sanctioned if other interventions fail to produce the desired effect.

Applying this approach in the case of a monopoly, I can argue that the Islamic economic framework would not outrightly reject a monopoly but would rather evaluate it from a public interest angle. In a contemporary sense, this public interest is a matter of harm done to consumers, or in other words, a monopoly may be assessed for its potential abuse of dominant position. If it is found that a monopoly is exploiting consumers, then appropriate legal action will be taken.

Al-Mawardi, a Shafi'i jurist (d. AH 450/AD 1058), has prescribed a method for price intervention:

> Imam should summon to a meeting all parties to price negotiation, i.e. the bid traders, buyers and other experts. Their opinions will be sought and assessment made on the rates at which they buy and sell in the market. An agreement will be reached on prices that [are] beneficial to the sellers and socially acceptable without coercion. Whosoever permitted price control would use this method.[28]

Notice that even in justifying state intervention in setting market prices, Al-Mawardi is so careful about imposing a price control that he stresses how the price negotiation must be free of coercion. Another point to be noted here is that the above method is prescribed only in a case in which the state resorts to price control; that is, this mutual consultation is neither required nor recommended under normal market conditions. When it

---

[28] Bashar, "Price Control in an Islamic Economy اقتصاد إسلامي في التسعير," 34.

comes to price controls, Islamic law clearly is very restrained in terms of allowing the state to intervene in market operations.

The other situations, such as coercion, cheating, or collusion, are civil matters; that is, they are considered crimes in a civil court and must be dealt with accordingly. If traders have resorted to collusive behavior, they should be, after due investigation, punished accordingly.

An overview of the above cases suggests that the Islamic state can resort to price control only in special circumstances. Even if this option must be considered, at least the state's intervention is conditioned with appropriate investigation about natural and true costs as well as the real conduct of merchants, something akin to a modern-day competition or antitrust investigation. Also, such a price control is strictly a temporary measure, and therefore all price controls must be lifted as soon as a situation is normalized.

When the Prophet established the institution of *hisbah* (market inspector), he delegated enforcement of this regulatory framework to this institute. One can readily observe the enforcement of such a framework by asking if it brought parity between trading parties as well as between producer and consumer. It should be emphasized that despite this comprehensive framework of business regulations, the Prophet did not introduce any form of price controls. Clearly for him, price controls were unfair by their very nature, and he quickly established norms—and legal boundaries—to remove unfairness from the business practices of his time. This provided a model of an essentially free market with a strong, rule-based regulatory regime.

3.4. GOLD, FIAT CURRENCY, AND CENTRAL BANKING

In pre-Islamic Arabia, the Byzantine gold *dinar*, Persian silver *dirhami*, and copper *fals* (or *fels*; pl. *falus* or *fulus*) were used as coins. The value of both dinar and dirham was determined by their metal content (but not the *fals*). Coinage was not issued by a government authority, and minting coins was in the hands of private individuals. Disputes regarding weight and quality caused loss of economic efficiency; it did, however, provide competition and thus consumer choice. In the early Islamic Empire, Muslims continued to use Byzantine coins, but over time they outlawed the use of these coins and centralized the production of an Islamic *dinar* and *dirham.* The circulation of the Islamic dinar expanded, as did the Islamic Empire. In the Ottoman Empire, major production centers of gold were controlled, which ensured that coins were not debased. Paper currency was introduced in the nineteenth century, along the lines of developments in Europe.

Abu Hamed Mohammad ibn Mohammad Ghazali, commonly known as Imam Ghazali (d. AH 505/AD 1111), the towering Islamic thinker and theologian, has addressed the issue of currency debasement.[29] During his time, this took the form of reducing the gold and silver content in coins, or simply "shaving" or "shedding" off some of the metals. For Ghazali, circulating one bad dirham was worse than stealing a thousand dirhams, for theft is committed once whereas circulating bad money steals from everyone who uses it. But, interestingly, Imam Ghazali accepted coins of mixed metals as licit, provided they were issued by the state.

Egyptian historian Al-Maqrizi (d. 845 AH/1442 AD) authored a work titled *Book of Aiding the Nation by Investigating the Depression* [of 1403–6].[30] In a published conference paper, Mark Tomass presents a translation and commentary on this important work that challenges the "great gap" hypothesis of Austrian-born

---

[29] Abdul Azim Islahi, "An Analytical Study of al-Ghazali's Thought on Money and Interest," 1, accessed November 20, 2019, https://mpra.ub.uni-muenchen.de/41438/.

[30] Mark Tomass, "Al-Maqrízi's *Book of Aiding the Nation by Investigating the Depression* of 1403–6: Translation and Commentary," in *Joseph A. Schumpeter, Historian of Economics: Selected Papers from the History of Economics Society Conference, 1994,* ed. Laurence S. Moss, Perspectives on the History of Economic Thought (London: Routledge, 1996), 110–54, https://doi.org/10.4324/9780203435977.

American economist Joseph Schumpeter.[31] A quote from Tomass is worth full attention:

> During the reign of Al-Zahir Barqouq [784–801/1382–99], the Ustadar Mahmoud ben Ali was appointed to manage the sultan's treasury. His appetite to profit and amass wealth was the cause for the excessive increase in the circulation of flous. He imported red copper from Europe and secured the mint in Cairo with an amount of money. Flous continued to be minted there during his appointment; he also took on a mint in Alexandria in order to produce flous. As a result, people's holding of flous increased considerably, and their circulation increased to become the dominant circulating money in the country.[32]

As this shows, Al-Maqrizi accurately foretold the ills associated with inflation and hyperinflation![33]

Ibn Taimiyah (d. 728/1328) had gone one step further by anticipating Gresham's law, which holds that bad money will drive out the good money whenever there were two different monetary units with the same face value but different intrinsic value in terms of precious metal content.[34] Ibn Taimiyah had

[31] Tomass, "Al-Maqrízi's *Book of Aiding the Nation by Investigating the Depression* of 1403–6." Schumpeter has argued that there is a gap of five hundred years in the history of economic thought prior to Thomas Aquinas (d. AH 273/AD 1274).

[32] Tomass, "Al-Maqrízi's *Book of Aiding the Nation by Investigating the Depression* of 1403–6," 129.

[33] The "great gap" hypothesis was the main topic of this book: S. M. Ghazanfar, ed., *Medieval Islamic Economic Thought: Filling the Great Gap in European Economics.* London: Taylor & Francis Books, 2003, https://doi.org/10.4324/9780203633700.

[34] Muhammad Aslam Haneef and Emad Rafiq Barakat, "Must Money Be Limited to Only Gold and Silver? A Survey of Fiqhi Opinions and Some Implications," *Journal of King Abdulaziz University–Islamic Economics* 19, no. 1 (2006), https://doi.org/10.4197/islec.19–1.2, 23.

defined the two main purposes of money as a store of value and as a medium of exchange. He was critical of debasement, melting of coins, trading of money, and excessive issuance of currency; he considered these measures harmful for general economic welfare. His arguments were echoed by calls from the modern-day Austrian school of economics for a return to a gold standard and 100 percent reserve banking.

Contemporary scholars of Islamic finance, for the most part, accept fiat currency (paper currency backed by a government decree). In a survey done to understand the views of Islamic finance scholars on fiat currency, 57 percent of scholars seem to approve fiat currency, whereas 11.5 percent disapprove of it, and the rest remain neutral. "In conclusion, based on this survey," write contemporary academics Syammon Jaffar, Adam Abdullah, and Ahamed Kameel Mydin Meera, "most of our *shari'ah* scholars were unaware of and confused by the mechanics of money creation, especially in respect of the issue of FRB (Fractional Reserve Banking) for both the conventional and Islamic banking systems."[35]

Malaysian academics Aslam Haneef and Emad Rafiq have done a review of jurists' opinion on paper money. They report that Mufti Taqi Usmani, a leading scholar of Islamic finance, represents the majority view that paper currency is licit. He believes that its conversion or redemption into gold or silver now serves no purpose. Furthermore, Taqi Usmani also holds that paper currency can be considered akin to *falus* (or *fulus*). He also considers currency trading licit given that the currencies involved differ.[36]

---

[35] Syammon Jaffar, Adam Abdullah, and Ahamed Kameel Mydin Meera, "Fiat Money: From the Current Islamic Finance Scholars' Perspective," *Humanomics* 33, no. 3 (August 14, 2017): 274–96, https://doi.org/10.1108/H-01-2017-0013.

[36] Haneef and Barakat, "Must Money Be Limited to Only Gold and Silver?"

In contrast, some scholars look at fiat currency with suspicion. Yusuf notes that "any (currency) issue without full reserve is gross betrayal of the ordinary man's confidence."[37] The historic US gold certificate is mentioned by some as a halal option (i.e., permissible by Islamic law). Others have argued that Islam recommends automatism and a kind of neutralizing of money and calls for adopting a gold standard and a universal currency instead of subjugating the currency to a government.

In their article surveying the opinions of Islamic jurists on the permissibility of fiat currency, Muhammad Aslam Haneef and Emad Rafiq Barakat, two contemporary academics, essentially present arguments on both sides.[38] They cite the prophetic approval of gold and silver to legitimize their use as a medium of exchange and store of value, but they also cite the lack of prohibition on any other forms of currency. In supporting the views of approval of fiat currency, Haneef and Barakat argue that it is not "practical" to restrict the currency to only gold and silver.[39] They report that currently, almost all Muslim scholars and jurists have approved the use of fiat currency.

Notwithstanding this general approval, fiat currency seems to fail in two basic parameters of Islamic law: equivalence in terms of weight (*mizan*) and volumes (*miqyal*), as the value of fiat currency varies over time. Imam al-Ghazali wrote, "It is the transgressor who mints the coins with difference in quality."[40] He also argued that "to put counterfeit money in circulation is of great injustice as all those who accept it are harmed."[41]

---

[37] Yusuf, *Economic Justice in Islam*, 51.

[38] Haneef and Barakat, "Must Money Be Limited to Only Gold and Silver?"

[39] Haneef and Barakat, "Must Money Be Limited to Only Gold and Silver?," 30–31.

[40] Quoted in Hifzur Rab, *Economic Justice in Islam: Monetary Justice and the Way Out of Interest (Riba)* (Kuala Lumpur, Malaysia: Noordeen, 2006), 180.

[41] Quoted in Rab, *Economic Justice in Islam*, 180.

Minting coins with a difference in quality is akin to a central bank printing equal value currency notes of different values or purchasing power. In a high-inflation environment, when the central bank prints more money, it only results in inflation and erosion of purchasing power by the masses. This act, Imam al-Ghazali would have said, is a transgression.

Contemporary scholar Hifzur Rab takes a similar position, while subjecting fiat currency to criticism. Favoring gold-backed currency, he argues, "Stability of money is an essential requirement of justice, and free people select [the] best available measure of wealth as a medium of exchange."[42]

It should also be noted, for the sake of clarity, that most money printed now is not issued by a central bank but rather by commercial banks through issuance of credit. Thus anyone with surplus capital has far easier access to credit than anyone else, which supports an argument that fiat currencies cause inequality.

In a truly Islamic economic system, banks will assume a limited role. They will not create money, as they normally do in a fractional reserve banking system. Rather, as "Islamic economics" scholars Mirakhor Askari, Zamir Iqbal, and Abbas Mirakhor explain, "financial institutions would be serving their traditional role of intermediation between savers and investors but with no debt on their balance sheets, no leveraging, and no predetermined interest rate payments as an obligation."[43] They relate this proposal to the Chicago Plan, which was formulated by a group of University of Chicago professors back in 1933.

In the contemporary world, these ideas have scant but serious following. One prominent example is Sheykh Umar Vadillo, a Muslim convert from Spain now based in Pakistan. In 1991, Umar Vadillo issued a "Fatwa on paper money" in which he declared that paper money is an instrument of *riba* (usury),

---

[42] Rab, *Economic Justice in Islam*, 161.

[43] Askari, Iqbal, and Mirakhor, *Introduction to Islamic Economics*, 203.

and *zakat* (obligatory tithe) cannot be paid with it.[44] A year later, in 1992, in Granada, Spain, Vadillo's community minted gold dinar coins, in accordance with the standard of the second caliph, Umar Ibn ul Khattab. This was the first of its kind since the abolishment of the Ottoman caliphate. At the same time, Vadillo founded the World Islamic Mint, World Islamic Trade Organisation, and online gold payment system "E-Dinar," thus making halal money and trade possible again.[45] His efforts may be utopian, but they reflect an Islamic uneasiness with fiat currency.

This uneasiness goes back to classical Islamic jurists who were deeply aware of the risks posed by debasement of currency. Historically, their financial analysis exposed the damage that currency debasement did to their economies, and they held their central governments responsible for this injustice. Modern economic literature arrives at the same conclusion. The world has abolished gold to underpin currency, but there is a strong case made in minority economic circles to revive a gold-backed monetary system.

It is difficult to take a clear position for a gold-backed currency based on Islamic precepts. What is clear for the Islamic economic framework, however, is that sound money holds central importance. It is also clear that the backing of a central bank or a federal government is subject to changes in geopolitics, leading to unsound money and great loss of wealth for currency holders. Today the dollar is strong; tomorrow the renminbi may be stronger. A stable government helps stabilize its exchange rate, but a change in the government brings

---

[44] Umar Vadillo, *Fatwa Concerning the Islamic Prohibition on Using Paper Money as a Medium of Exchange* (Granada, Spain: Madinah, 1991). Note that the term *fatwa* literally means "an opinion." In the Islamic tradition, fatwa is a religious opinion given by Islamic scholars based on the foundations of Islamic knowledge. But a fatwa is not legally binding.

[45] Personal communication with Shaykh Umar Vadillo, August 2018, Lahore.

instability. Therefore, an external benchmark for currency valuation, which may or may not be gold, sounds like a better economic policy. This valuation should also consider such factors as production levels when assessing the actual economic situation in a country.

3.5. *RIBA* AND AN ISLAMIC ALTERNATIVE

If there is one topic that has received the most attention by writers about "Islamic economics," it is charging interest on loans because this is considered absolutely forbidden in Islam. The Qur'an uses the word *riba* (usury) for this practice and vehemently prohibits it:

> Those that live on usury shall rise up before God like men whom Satan has demented by his touch; for they claim that trading is no different from usury. But God has permitted trading and made usury unlawful. He that has received an admonition from his Lord and mended his ways may keep his previous gains; God will be his judge. Those that turn back shall be the inmates of the Fire, wherein they shall abide for ever. (2:275)

While there is consensus today among Islamic scholars that charging interest on cash loans with the intent of receiving a predetermined profit is *haram* (forbidden), what is not agreed on is the definition of *riba* and the application of that definition in the current financial system. For instance, some modern-day scholars do extend the application of *riba* to banking interest, whereas others do not. This section will review some of the major contributions to this controversy by Islamic economists, jurists, and theologians including Abbas Mirakhor, Javed Ahmad Ghamidi, Muhammad Akram Khan, Imran Ahsan Khan Nyazee, and Fazlur Rahman, though not in this order.

Contemporary "Islamic economics" scholars Askari, Iqbal, and Mirakhor refer to *riba* as the "premium that must be paid by the borrower to the lender along with the principal amount as a condition of the loan or for an extension in the duration of loan."[46] They identify at least four characteristics to define *riba*:

1. It is positive and fixed *ex ante*.
2. It is tied to the time period and the amount of the loan.
3. Its payment is guaranteed regardless of the outcome or the purposes for which the principal loan was borrowed.
4. The state apparatus sanctions and enforces its collection.[47]

In my opinion, the fourth characteristic that the authors identify is additional, as indeed *riba* can occur as a contract between two private parties with or without the involvement of the state.

In his book *Mizan*, Pakistani theologian Javed Ahmad Ghamidi defines this term as follows: "[*Riba*] implies a fixed increase which a lender demands from the borrower just because he has given him the permission to use his money for a certain period."[48]

The basic rationale for the prohibition of *riba* that Muslim jurists and experts of Islamic finance offer can be summarized as follows. The basic element of a buy-and-sell transaction (*al-bay*, 'an "exchange") is sharing risk between two parties. In the case of money lending with a profit agreed on in advance, this element of risk sharing is eliminated, and the entire risk of the transaction shifts to the borrower.[49] Islam considers that borrowing for business or consumption needs is a legitimate necessity and does not discourage borrowing as such. This is

---

[46] Askari, Iqbal, and Mirakhor, *Introduction to Islamic Economics*, 81.

[47] Askari, Iqbal, and Mirakhor, *Introduction to Islamic Economics*, 81–82.

[48] Ghamidi, *Islam*, 474.

[49] It can be argued, though, that even in this case of lending money with a pre-agreed profit, the lender still assumes the risk—of losing his money. But we are talking about a scenario in which the loan has been secured through personal guarantees and collaterals.

also evident from the longest verse of the Qur'an (2:282), which discusses the case of loan contracts and affirms the importance of obtaining proper written documentation as well as witnesses if possible. Likewise, the next verse (v. 283) discusses the case of a verbal loan contract and affirms the importance of giving a token or pledge as evidence. The lending must be at essentially zero-interest rate, however, without stipulation of a fixed time period for repayment.

Contemporary Lebanese academic Ayman Reda has emphasized the Qur'anic distinction between *riba* and trade. He writes that "the difference lies in the nature of exchange taking place. Where trade involves the exchange of goods for money or other goods, usury is the exchange of one commodity for the same commodity with an increase in the repayment."[50] Reda makes a fine point by arguing that "trade allows humans to exchange their 'excess property' in an attempt to satisfy any deficiencies on both sides."[51]

A leading contemporary Pakistani jurist Imran Ahsan Khan Nyazee, in his treatise *The Prohibition of Riba Elaborated*, has provided extensive commentaries while applying the classical understanding of *fiqh* on modern banking and finance transactions.[52] Nyazee views that in principle, a loan transaction is considered void in Islamic law unless it is a *qard hasan* (loan given out of compassion without expectation of a benefit). He not only considers cash loans as usurious but also deems time deposits in banks as well as financial transactions involving delayed payment as void. Nyazee also considers an interest-free loan to a bank as void, as it extends undue benefits to the

---

[50] Ayman Reda, "Islam and Markets," *Review of Social Economy* 71, no. 1 (March 1, 2013): 29, https://doi.org/10.1080/00346764.2012.761752.

[51] Reda, "Islam and Markets," 29.

[52] Imran Ahsan Khan Nyazee, *The Prohibition of Riba Elaborated*, Islamic Banking Series 1 (Islamabad, Pakistan: Advanced Legal Studies Institute, 2009).

bank. Moreover, he is also opposed to the option of service charges. In other words, in Nyazee's opinion, the whole edifice of Islamic banking and finance is legally void.

A major criticism of Islamic banking comes from former auditor Muhammad Akram Khan, who is also from Pakistan and has retired from government service. In his book *What Is Wrong with Islamic Economics?* he has written an extensive and comprehensive review of debate on *riba* in classical and modern Islamic scholars.[53] Khan essentially rejects the conceptual foundations of both "Islamic economics" and "Islamic finance"—models that consider all interest as illicit. In his commentary on *riba*, Khan maintains that orthodox Muslim scholars have not differentiated between a loan and a financing transaction, which has led them to erroneously include all types of interest under *riba*. He defines *riba* as "any increment on the principal sum of a loan."[54] He calls his readers' attention to "a need to revert to the original and pristine definition of the term '*riba*' and keep it restricted to loan transactions. Interest on transactions of financing and investment should not be covered by '*riba*.'"[55]

Khan provides useful examples to differentiate between lending (with or without interest) and financing. While he recognizes that there is a consensus that an increment on the principal sum of a loan is *riba*, he stresses that not all financial transactions arise from loan transactions. Khan gives several examples: "Financial claims could arise through trade (e.g. credit sale), investment (e.g. share certificates), provision of services (e.g. transportation of goods, renting of buildings), recovery of an earlier overpayment, project financing and so on."[56]

---

[53] Muhammad Akram Khan, *What Is Wrong with Islamic Economics?: Analysing the Present State and Future Agenda*, Studies in Islamic Finance, Accounting and Governance (Cheltenham, UK: Edward Elgar, 2013).

[54] Khan, *What Is Wrong with Islamic Economics?*, 242.

[55] Khan, *What Is Wrong with Islamic Economics?*, xvi.

[56] Khan, *What Is Wrong with Islamic Economics?*, 226.

Like Nyazee, Khan is critical of the emergence of Islamic banks and Islamic financial institutions and considers them "ruses" and "subterfuge" to hide behind terms while still charging interest. He maintains that the modern banking system has evolved considerably over the last three hundred years, and effectively this type of financing did not exist at the time of the Prophet Muhammad. When banks are essentially in the financing business and not in the lending business and they charge interest on financing services, this interest cannot be termed as *riba*. In the same sense, anyone who makes deposits in a bank has not lent the money but merely deposited it for return and safety; hence, the question of *riba* does not arise. In other words, modern-day banking is Islamically permissible.

Fazlur Rahman (d. 1988), a key "modernist" thinker in Islam over the past century, in his masterpiece "Ribā and Interest," maintained a different stance.[57] He argued that the Qur'an contrasts *riba* with *sadaqa* (2:275), a term he translates as "cooperation and mutual consideration."[58] He added that this spirit of cooperation needs to be rekindled before abolishing banking interest altogether. Rahman believes that in its original spirit, Islam viewed then-prevalent *riba* as contrary to this spirit of mutual cooperation. Thus, he offers a practical solution before outrightly abolishing the institution of bank interest, a solution that can provide services like credit when needed with a voluntary spirit.

In 2002, in reply to the query of Arab Banking Corporation, one of the most respected religious authorities in the Islamic world, Shaykh-ul-Azhar Dr. Muhammad Sayyid Tantawi (d. 2010) of Al-Azhar University in Cairo, Egypt, issued a fatwa (religious opinion) permitting earning of fixed profits on banking deposits. The fatwa concludes as follows:

---

[57] Fazlur Rahman, "Ribā and Interest," *Islamic Studies* 3, no. 1 (March 1964): 1–43, www.jstor.org/stable/20832724.

[58] Rahman, "Ribā and Interest," 32.

In summary, prespecification of profits for those who invest their funds through an investment agency with banks or other institutions is legally permissible, and above legal suspicion. This transaction belongs to the domain of benefits that were neither explicitly permitted nor explicitly forbidden and does not belong to the domains of creeds or formal acts of worship, wherein change and alteration is not allowed.[59]

Al-Azhar University's fatwa argues that the relationship between the depositor and the banker is that of an investor and investee, and therefore it is legitimate to earn a profit on one's investment. One obvious caveat, however, is that in this case there is no chance of a loss, unlike in a conventional business investment in which the investors assume chance of both profit and loss. In the case of making a bank deposit, the only uncertainty is over the rate of return, and not whether this return will be positive or negative.

Currently, Ghamidi is of the opinion that pure money-based lending from banks has almost vanished, with the exception of credit card financing. He believes that now all banks operate in the mode of financing and not lending, and thus while he remains opposed to *riba*, he does not consider most of the banking finance transactions as *riba*. This has addressed some of the fundamental concerns raised by Islamic economists.

In other words, there are scholars who argue that modern banking interest is legitimate from an Islamic point of view. But many others disagree, seeing modern banking interest as the very *riba* that the Qur'an condemns. This latter view has led to the rise of an Islamic alternative to an interest-based banking

---

[59] Shaykh-ul-Azhar Dr. Muhammad Sayyid Tantawi, as quoted in Naveed Mohammed, "Al Azhar University Fatwa Allows for Fixed Returns on Bank Deposits," Islamic Finance Foundation/Sukuk.com (website), March 20, 2014, https://www.sukuk.com/education/al-azhar-university-fatwa-interest-bank-deposits-271/.

system in the form of Islamic banks and financial institutions. It may be worth attention that before a puritan version of "Islamic banks," Muslim banks emerged which operated like conventional banks in all aspects.[60]

This notion of "Islamic finance" intends to develop a system in which risks of losses, just like expectations of profits, can be shared between financiers and borrowers, while it is assumed that the borrowers can be both businesspeople in need of capital for business as well as ordinary people. Thus it offers a risk-sharing model as a substitute for conventional banking, which is interest based.

Khan argues that in the case of Islamic finance, however, "profit-loss sharing poses insurmountable problems of accounting and monitoring in practice, making it impossible to practice it at a global basis.... The theoretical concept of profit-loss sharing (which is not practicable) makes a weak case of Islamic finance."[61]

A related discussion in Islamic finance is fractional reserve banking and the risks imposed by creation of assets literally out of thin air. It is believed that under an Islamic economy, banking will be 100 percent reserve based, and fractional reserve banking will be undone. Ideally, banking assets should be backed by

---

[60] Michael O'Sullivan unearths the emergence and evolution of 'Muslim banks' during the first half of the twentieth century in the parts of Ottoman Empire, including Bosnia and India, which charged interest and operated like conventional banks, and aimed at a Muslim economic renaissance, in an insightful article: "Interest, Usury, and the Transition from 'Muslim' to 'Islamic' Banks, 1908–1958." *International Journal of Middle East Studies* 52 (2020): 261–287, https://doi.org/10.1017/S0020743820000239. Islamic authorities endorsed these banks saying "amounts taken and given, as well as the deposits, loans, debts, and transactions at the aforementioned bank, and the increase in interest thereby obtained (by means of lending and borrowing) is legitimate and permissible." These Muslim banks could not survive due to competition as long as pressure from religious groups.

[61] Khan, *What Is Wrong with Islamic Economics?*, 237–38.

gold to minimize the fluctuation in the value of the nominal currency that is tied to movements in the prices of gold itself, which changes rather slowly. I have already addressed this issue earlier in this chapter.[62]

In his book *Economic Justice in Islam*, Rab makes an important point while referring to the authority of Imam Abu Yusuf (d. AH 181/AD 798), one of the prominent disciples of Imam Abu Hanifa (d. AH 150/AD 767). In their time, two currencies were prevalent in the Islamic Empire: the gold dinar and copper falus (or fulus), with an exchange rate. Imam Yusuf believed that any loan contract underwritten, say in falus, had to be equated with the prevalent value of gold. At the time of return, the borrower must return the falus to obtain the same value of gold. This implicitly acknowledged the time-value concept of money and protected the lender's assets by underwriting the loan transaction with the more stable gold.[63]

Interest rate as a monetary policy tool and interest charged on loans are interrelated but are also two separate concepts. It can be established without any doubt that Islam does not allow lenders to charge interest on cash loans. This prohibition is the same regardless of the interest rate, purpose of the loan, and financial status of the beneficiary. On the other hand, there seems to be less clarity among Islamic economists about how modern commercial banks create money due to fractional reserve banking. This is done on the back of a central bank, which relies on a discount rate for credit allocation preferences. For Islamic economists, fiat currency, banks (once they have been Islamized), and the financial system Islamized banks create are legitimate. But this is an area in which more research is needed both on empirical and legal grounds.

We should understand that banks have evolved over centuries, and in their social evolution, they have addressed several

---

[62] See discussion under sec. 3.4, "Gold, Fiat Currency, and Central Banking."

[63] Rab, *Economic Justice in Islam*, 206.

shortcomings in their model. As a part of this evolution, they have also brought down interest rates significantly and now even operate at zero or even negative interest rates. Under an Islamic economy, banks, as they function today, will take deposits, undertake trading and investment, and provide financing facilities. As these functions entail provision of services while incurring costs, there will be a price tag, which can be a combination of fee, interest, and share in the profit/loss, depending on the nature of the contract. Therefore, we do not need a separate "Islamic banking" system, and modern banking infrastructure is able to provide these services except in the case of explicit interest-bearing cash loans, which will be prohibited. Other forms of nonbanking, *riba* transactions will also be disallowed.

3.6. ISLAMIC FISCAL POLICY

The modern nation-state, at least in democratic societies, draws the power of taxation from the people. Hence, any tax-related matters are presented in a house of elected members and then converted into legislation, after which they are implemented. Muslim societies and countries are no exception to this. The debate about the limits of the government is one of the most important in both economics and political science. In politics, and in the context of democratic discourse, the reference is often made to the rights of individuals versus the rights of the state. Economic freedom in particular concerns itself with the size of the government. In theory, economic freedom increases as the size of the government decreases, and hence this literature calls for a minimum level of government intervention, which should lead to prosperity. Whether the realm is political or economic, the power of the government—and the corresponding power of the individual—ultimately depend on the degree of taxation. The institutions that a government normally creates to enforce its authority (e.g., police and courts) are also ultimately financed by the tax that citizens pay. Taxation is the source of all power that the modern state has acquired and continues to hold.

For conceptual understanding, let's consider two extreme cases: the first with a 0 percent tax and the second with a 100 percent tax. We can say that in a society in which the government on the one hand imposes a 0 percent tax, there will be no government; you will rather have anarchy. On the other hand, in a society in which the government imposes a 100 percent tax, ultimately everything will be government owned. In a way, there will be no free citizen or any private property. Obviously, in a real world, the tax rate—and corresponding power of the government—will lie somewhere on this spectrum.

As the Qur'an mentions *zakat* (an obligatory, annual, rule-based deduction from wealth) as many times as it mentions *salat* (daily prayers, five times a day), Muslims are deeply aware of this financial transaction that is one of the five pillars of Islam. *Zakat* is an annual obligatory payment on the assets of Muslims over a threshold level, provided they are free of encumbrance. This threshold level, called *nisabi*, was originally defined as follows:

1. *Wealth*: 642 grams of silver
2. *Produce*: 653 kilograms of dates
3. *Livestock*: 5 camels, 30 cows, 40 goats

In the year 2019, *nisab* has been calculated equivalent to US $3,849.

Zakat is collected annually on wealth of all sorts, produce of all forms, and livestock of all types from every Muslim citizen who is liable to it. As Ghamidi explains, its rates are as follows:

1. Wealth: 2.5 percent annually
2. Produce:
   - 5 percent on all items that are produced by the interaction of both labor and capital
   - 10 percent on items that are produced such that the basic factor in producing them is either labor or capital
   - 20 percent on items that are produced neither as a result of capital nor labor but actually are a gift of God
3. Livestock: variable rates[64]

What will the state do with the taxes it has collected? The Qur'an gives an answer by categorizing (9:60) the expenditures on which *zakat* can be spent as follows:

1. الْفُقَرَاءِ وَالْمَسَاكِينِ (*al-fuqara' wa al-masakin*): the poor and the needy;

2. الْعَامِلِينَ عَلَيْهَا (*al-'amilina 'alayha*): the salaries of all employees of the state;

3. الْمُؤَلَّفَةِ قُلُوبُهُمْ (*al-mu'allafat-I qulubuhum*): all political expenditures in the interest of Islam and the Muslims;

4. فِي الرِّقَابِ (*fi al-riqab*): for liberation of slaves;

5. الْغَارِمِينَ (*al-gharimin*): for helping people who are suffering economic losses or are burdened with a fine or a loan;

6. فِي سَبِيلِ اللَّهِ (*fi sabilillah*): for serving Islam and for the welfare of citizens; and

7. ابْنِ السَّبِيلِ (*ibn al-sabil*): for helping travelers and for the construction of roads, bridges, and rest houses for these travelers.

Furthermore, Islamic law considers the following as exemptions from *zakat*:

1. tools of production, trade, and business;
2. personal items of daily use; and
3. a fixed quantity called nisab, which can be understood as the threshold below which zakat is not collected.

Historically speaking, the Islamic state did not depend on *zakat* only. It collected *al-jizya*, an equivalent protection tax from non-Muslims living in Muslim lands against services and protection and also exempting them from jihad. It also collected *al-kharaj*, an annual land-produce tax from non-Muslims from when Muslims conquered other nations but those lands were not confiscated, and the original owners of these conquered nations were allowed to keep cultivating against an annual payment on produce. During the time of the second caliph of Islam, 'Umar bin al-Khattab imposed a countervailing and reciprocal duty to the extent of 10 percent on merchants conducting trade in Muslim lands. In addition, *al-rakaz* was also collected, which was a tax on minerals and sea fortune, to the tune of 20 percent.

Muhammad, the Prophet of Islam, was content with a frugal standard of living, even though as commander in chief he was entitled to 20 percent of war booty. He divided his entitlement into five portions, applying four-fifths to support the *ummah* (community) and reserving only one-fifth for his own family. In other words, he actually paid 80 percent of his own income share for general welfare, whereas the rate of *zakat* that applied to everyone else was from 2.5 to 20 percent.

Traditionally, *zakat* has always been understood as a religious obligation, differentiated from tax, that an Islamic state can impose. This is captured in the details in this fatwa by the contemporary Saudi jurist Shaykh Muhammad Saalih al-Munajjid.[65] But the same fatwa considers all taxes *haraam* (not permissible), except when the Islamic state needs to fulfill its needs and lacks financial resources. This inevitably opens the door to taxation beyond any limits, however, as the state can easily define any needs on the basis of its programs. For example, if a state undertakes a commercial project, it can impose a tax and claim legitimacy on the basis of this "need."

Considering *zakat* a purely religious obligation and tax a purely worldly obligation creates the sort of duality that Islam, being a comprehensive code of life, otherwise discourages. If we look at the eight designated heads of *zakat* again, we can find that none of the eight prescribed allocations is meant for a purely religious cause, whereas "religious" here is meant in the sense of arrangement of the masjid (mosque) and other rituals. Allah obliges Muslims to pay this "tax" not for His benefit but for people at large. It is different from prayers and fasting, which Muslims do for the sake of Allah alone. In fact, this social dimension of *zakat* is used today to find its new uses or new interpretation.

In today's Sudan, a security portfolio has been created through a partnership between Diwan Zakah (apex body of *zakat* management) and commercial banks. With a capital of 200 million pounds, the program provides insurance against genuine defaults by the clients of commercial banks at the second level. While the first level of default is covered by the personal guarantee of the client, this provides a useful example of how the interpretation of *al-gharimin* (people under debt) has been extended beyond just poor people.[66]

---

65 Muhammad Saalih al-Munajjid, "What Is the Difference between Zakaah and Taxes, and Is It Permissible to Impose Taxes? Is It Obligatory to Pay Them?," Islam Question & Answer (website), September 30, 2013, https://islamqa.info/en/answers /130920/the-difference-between-zak aah-and-taxes-and-the-conditions-of-imposing-taxes.

66 Abdullah et al., *Islamic Economics*, 712.

This discussion leads us to consider *zakat* as a part of transaction law, or *muamalat*,[67] instead of rituals. This changes the whole paradigm about *zakat*. Akram Khan makes this bold proposition that traditional Muslim scholars have erred by classifying *zakat* as an *ibadah* (devotional law) while it should have been classified as a transaction law.[68] He notes that several scholars have already indicated the need to redefine several important concepts concerning *zakat* such as exemption limits, rates, and scope. Khan indicates that one corollary of literal interpretation of *zakat* in the modern context is an inevitable inequity between different socioeconomic classes. For example, traditional scholars hold that income from businesses, salaries, and other means is exempt from *zakat*, whereas it is payable on the year-end savings in terms of cash, jewelry, and stock-in-trade.

Ghamidi believes that God has taken away the power of taxation from the government. He believes that Islam legitimizes only two forms of tax revenue: *zakat* and land use tax. He invokes the Qur'an for *zakat* and references the practice of both the Prophet and the early caliphs for the land use tax. But he does not limit the rate of *zakat* to only the usual 2.5 percent of net annual wealth, and he expands the scope of *zakat* to include all sources of income under different rates. Another major point of departure is Ghamidi's belief that the salaries of all state functionaries should be paid through *zakat*. He argues that it is the Islamic state that has sole authority to impose and collect these taxes.[69]

Ghamidi's theology on limiting the taxation powers of government is powerful. This can be used as an argument to challenge the authority of government, whether it is autocratic or democratic, an appealing prospect for Muslim democrats. In a

---

[67] Islamic law is classified as *ibadat* (devotional or religious rituals such as praying, fasting, etc.) and *muamalat* (transactions in civil and commercial matters).

[68] Khan, *What Is Wrong with Islamic Economics?*, 417.

[69] Ghamidi, *Islam*, 332.

recent working paper, the Turkish American economist Timur Kuran makes a similar argument.[70] He writes,

> The Islamic state that emerged under Muhammad's leadership ... could have raised taxes in an arbitrary way, expropriating assets at will when and where it saw them ... Instead, it instituted a predictable, fixed, and mildly progressive tax system designed to finance specific causes. Called zakat, the transfer system was considered sufficiently central to early Islam to be included among Islam's canonical five pillars.[71]

It is clear that a redefinition of *zakat* and reinterpretation of its heads significantly changes the public finance debate in Islam. On the one hand, *zakat* calculated at the flat rate of 10 percent on people's salaries, for example, provides a steady stream of income to the government. On the other hand, it also removes the arbitrary power of the government to increase this rate of taxation. It is worth an empirical analysis to determine how this stream of religiously inspired taxation can incentivize the tax payment in Muslim countries. In any case, reinterpretation of *zakat* makes a *zakat*-financed public system certainly feasible.

To summarize this discussion, *zakat* is applicable on both income and wealth, irrespective of sources of income. In the case of income calculation, *nisab* will be deducted before levying *zakat*, and in the case of wealth, no such deduction will be made if the condition of *nisab* is fulfilled. *Zakat* on yield of assets will be 10 percent, whereas it will be 5 percent in the case of human effort. The same applies to business, salaries, and

---

[70] Timur Kuran, "Zakat: Islam's Missed Opportunity to Limit Predatory Taxation," SSRN Scholarly Paper, Economic Research Initiatives at Duke (ERID) Working Paper No. 284 (Rochester, NY: Social Science Research Network, April 8, 2019), 1–32, https://dx.doi.org/10.2139/ssrn.3368292.

[71] Kuran, "Zakat," 24.

professional practice. As practicing and law-abiding Muslims pay both taxes and *zakat*, this anomaly needs to be removed. A simple solution is available: deduct *zakat* paid from income tax paid, thus giving Muslims a benefit. As a matter of fact, the Malaysian government has already institutionalized this by allowing *zakat* paid to prescribed government foundations to be deducted from the income tax payable.

The main message here is that under its economic framework, *shari'ah* provides a mechanism for public finance management; it has not been developed over time, however, restricting *zakat* to a very narrow purpose of relief for the poor. The low and flat rates of *zakat* leave businesses and professionals alike with higher disposable incomes that they can invest or consume as needed. The low rates of these Islamic taxes also keep a check on the size of the government, and once we accept the divine origin of these rates, then we can also provide a much-desired certainty to taxpayers about their liabilities. One obvious advantage of a *shari'ah*-compliant government, in this case, will be that this fiscal policy will not be alterable by government functionaries and elected politicians. If the principle of *nisab* is applied widely, then we can argue against imposition of sales tax or a value-added tax, as everyone irrespective of income has to pay some amount of tax at an equal rate. A society will be better off by allowing its economically poor segments to save more and to spend more rather than having to part with a portion of their wealth in the form of a government-administrated tax.

A government that depends on *zakat* collection, in which rates range from 2.5 percent to 20 percent of wealth, and on land value taxation will inevitably be limited and indeed relatively small. An Islamic state cannot demand any other tax payment from its citizens without their consent. This is because in Islam, the state is limited by God's commandments, and the usual powers of taxation that are available to modern governments under one pretext or another are severely curtailed. This is the religious doctrine of limited government. The size of a thus limited government will be capped at a maximum of

20 percent of national income drawing from the highest possible rate of *zakat*.

In 1879, the American economist Henry George suggested taxing the rent on the unimproved value of land. It can be argued that this is consistent with the Islamic approach. In fact, George proposed to replace all taxes with a single land value tax. In 2009, using this theory, it was estimated that in the United States, such a tax would yield an annual tax of US $2.5 trillion, assuming rental value of 5 percent of capital value of market, which was 40 percent of total government expenditure at that point. This is very significant as it means that land value tax alone can finance complete government expenditure as long as it is limited in size. The American government is bloated in size now, reaching to almost 40 percent of GDP. A government to the tune of 20 percent of the GDP can be easily financed by land value tax alone.[72]

Similarly, the potential of *zakat* collection can be surprising. It has been estimated, based on historical data available, that total *zakat* payable in Malaysia in 2004 was RM 27.586 billion (US $7.259 billion according to the then exchange rate), whereas the Malaysian government collected total tax revenue of RM 75.51 billion in the same year. Thus, *zakat* alone, if collected directly by the state, would have generated one-third of the total tax revenue.[73]

To conclude, I argue that *zakat* is not only a tax but a low and flat tax; it also has the potential of fulfilling several social needs. It can be argued that an Islamic fiscal policy, and the

---

[72] Pierre Lemieux, "Land Taxes: The Return of Henry George," The Library of Economics and Liberty, accessed March 25, 2020, https:// www.econlib.org/land-taxes-the-return-of-henry-george/.

[73] I am grateful to my colleagues Muhammad Adli Amirullah and Sabrina for providing these estimates based on the study by Nasim Shah Shirazi and Md. Fouad Bin Amin, "Prospects of Poverty Elimination through Potential Zakat Collection in OIC-Member Countries: Reappraised," *Journal of Islamic Economics, Banking and Finance* 6, no. 3 (2010): 55–74.

attendant public finance management, will be highly transparent, stable, and simple. In its most basic form, this policy will comprise taxes on assets and income at flat rates; it also will include a land value tax to be imposed on unimproved land to the extent of the implicit rental income, not exceeding 10 percent of the total value, according to the rates of *ushr*. Furthermore, all public goods, such as infrastructure, will be financed through land value tax, and all public and social services will be financed through *zakat* and other sources like *waqf*, to which we turn now.

3.7. WAQF—SOCIAL PROTECTION OF PEOPLE BY PEOPLE

In *shari'ah*, a *waqf* is a voluntary, permanent, irrevocable dedication of a portion of one's wealth in cash or in kind to Allah, typically allocated for a defined religious or charitable cause. The Prophet Muhammad himself introduced a permanent source of income for a predefined charitable purpose, having observed this practice in a Jewish tribe and adopting it as an Islamic institution of welfare.

The Prophet has said,

> When a person dies, his deeds are cut off except for three: continuing charity, knowledge that others benefitted from him, and a righteous son [or daughter)] who supplicates for him. (Al-Tirmidhi, hadith no. 1376)[74]

During the Muslim civilization's golden age from the eighth to thirteenth centuries AD, *waqf* properties proliferated across Muslim territories. These endowments were ring-fenced from government interference.

In his essay "Welfare beyond the State: 'Ihsani' Societal-Based Welfare," Malaysian politician and scholar Maszlee Malik writes

---

[74] Al-Tirmidhi, *Jami' al-Tirmidhi*, "What Has Been Related about a Waqf," accessed March 22, 2020, https://sunnah.com/tirmidhi/15/57.

that "the *waqf* was identified as a civil society institution developed by early Muslim societies that enabled people to resist vigorously any attempts by the state to take over the wealth of individuals."[75] For him, "A waqf is the most important institution for enshrining the Islamic ethos, balancing private ownership and communal obligations."[76]

In his pathbreaking book *Early Islam and the Birth of Capitalism*, Koehler has traced the historical evolution of *waqf* through the Prophet's times.[77] Prophet Muhammad had assigned the lands obtained after the conquest of Khaybar practically as a trust by assigning the revenues obtained from those lands for specific purposes for which 'Umar bin al-Khattab was a custodian or trustee. Koehler notes that following the examples set by the Prophet, Caliph Abu Bakar created a family trust fund by assigning income from his property to his family members. Caliphs 'Umar and Ali had assigned the income of their properties to a waqf in which the whole Muslim *ummah* (community) was the declared beneficiary. It is to be noted that the caliph 'Umar, who expanded the boundaries of the Islamic Empire several times over and who as caliph was entitled to 20 percent of war booty, assigned his claim to be used for general welfare.

Historical evidence shows that the *waqf*, along with *zakat*, for centuries contributed to economic well-being and social protection in Muslim societies. The *waqf* contributed to the flourishing of mosques, orphanages, motels, schools, sufi lodges, water wells, food distribution, and debt relief, to name several examples. Incidentally, non-Muslims could also benefit from a *waqf* (provided they were not at war), and in this way were

---

[75] Maszlee Malik, "Welfare beyond the State: 'Ihsani' Societal-Based Welfare," in *Islamic Foundations of a Free Society*, ed. Nouh El Harmouzi and Linda Whetstone, Hobart Paper 183 (London: Institute of Economic Affairs, 2016), 63, https://iea.org.uk/wp-content/uploads/2016/10/Islamic-Foundations-of-a-Free-Society.pdf.

[76] Malik, "Welfare beyond the State," 64.

[77] Koehler, *Early Islam and the Birth of Capitalism*, chapter 14.

provided an alternative means to receive welfare given that as non-Muslims they were not entitled to receive *zakat*. In sum, the *waqf* system enabled civil society to flourish as an independent entity from the state. According to the contemporary Bangladeshi scholar Md. Thowhidul Islam, "From its inception, *Waqf* has been an integral part of the development of every Muslim society wherever it was established."[78] He writes, "In Algeria about half of the cultivable land was endowed as *Waqf* in the mid of 19th century, while it was one third in Tunis [as recorded in] 1883, three fourth in the Turkish [Ottoman] Empire (1928) and about one seventh in Egypt (1935) and Iran (1930)."[79]

During colonization, in many Muslim countries, the *waqf* properties were taken over by the state, which led to a fundamental change in their governance model. This trend of government control continued after the independence of these countries and the institution of *waqf* lost its social and economic significance.[80]

Waqf may be categorized according to the nature of their beneficiaries into these types: religious *waqf*, which is meant for mosques and religious schools and associated properties; philanthropic *waqf*, which aims at helping the poor segments; and family *waqf*, which is dedicated for the children and descendants of the *waqif*, the individual who sets up a *waqf*. Another categorization is possible depending on the type of underlying asset: a physical *waqf* is usually in the form of real estate, and a cash *waqf* is where the underlying assets are monetary in nature.[81]

---

[78] Md. Thowhidul Islam, *Historical Development of Waqf Governance in Bangladesh: Challenges and Prospects*, in *Building an Islamic Case for Open Markets*, ed. Ali Salman and Husnul Amin (Islamabad, Pakistan: IRD, 2019), 310.

[79] Islam, *Historical Development of Waqf*, 315.

[80] Islam, *Historical Development of Waqf*, 316.

[81] Abdullah et al., *Islamic Economics*, 714.

3.8. LAW OF INHERITANCE

It is remarkable to note that while the Qur'an has only described broad principles about economic policy, it has mentioned an explicit formula for the distribution of inheritance. There is a strong rationale for this divine guidance: in the matter of inheritance, feelings of individuals and prevalent circumstances are likely to influence distribution, which can result in injustice—and certainly also in dispute.

An overview of this distribution mechanism, as elaborated in Qur'an, is as follows:

1. If the deceased has outstanding debts to his name, then first of all they should be paid off from the wealth he has left behind. After this, any will he may have bequeathed should be paid. The distribution of his inheritance should then follow.

2. No will can be made in favor of an heir ordained by the Almighty except if his circumstances, or the services rendered by him or his needs in certain situations call for it. Similarly, a person who has severed the founda-tions of kinship with a person through his words and deeds cannot be his heir.

3. After giving the parents and the spouses their shares, the children are the heirs of the remaining inheritance. If the deceased does not have any male offspring and there are only two or more girls among the children, then they shall receive two-thirds of the inheritance left over, and if there is only one girl, then her share is one-half. If the deceased has only male children, then all his wealth shall be distributed among them. If he leaves behind both boys and girls, then the share of each boy shall be equal to the share of two girls and, in this case also, all his wealth shall be distributed among them.

4. In the absence of children, the deceased's brothers and sisters shall take their place. After giving the parents and spouses their shares, the brothers and sisters shall be his heirs. The proportion of their shares and the mode of distribution shall be the same as that of the children stated above.

5. If the deceased has children or if he does not have children and has brothers and sisters, then the parents shall receive one-sixth each. If he does not even have brothers and sisters and the parents are the sole heirs, then one-third of his wealth shall be given to the mother and two-thirds to the father.

6. If the deceased is a man and he has children, then his wife shall receive one-eighth of what he leaves, and if he does not have any children, then his wife's share shall be one-fourth. If the deceased is a woman and does not have any children, then her husband shall receive one-half of what she leaves and if she has children, then the husband's share is one-fourth.

7. In the absence of these heirs, the deceased can make someone an heir. If the person who is made an heir is a relative and has one brother or one sister, then they shall be given one-sixth of his share and he himself shall receive the remaining five-sixths. However, if he has more than one brother or sister, then they shall be given one-third of his share and he himself shall receive the remaining two-thirds.[82]

The state cannot claim inheritance and hence cannot impose inheritance tax in Islam. The only exception is a situation in which there are no direct or indirect relatives present to claim an inheritance, in which case the inheritance escheats to the state treasury. The details provided in Qur'an about inheritance

---

[82] Quoted from Ghamidi, *Islam*, 485–86.

allocation serve as a guideline to ensure that the inheritance is not a matter of discretion but follows rules. As a matter of fact, only one-third of property can be written in a will, limiting the concept of private property.[83]

---

[83] For an earlier discussion of this limitation of wealth circulation and distribution relating to inheritance, see toward the end of sec. 2.3, "Wealth Circulation."

4

Islamic Economic Framework: Historical Romance or Practical Prescription?

E ven if one agrees with the principles and institutional makeup presented here, there is a key first question to answer, plus several related questions: Is an Islamic vision of economic liberty an intellectual romanticization, or something that can be put into practice today? Do Islamic principles solve the myriad economic problems in today's interconnected, globalized world? Do they address challenges such as unemployment, inequality, and sustainable development? Can these institutions emerge or develop in societies in which corruption, authoritarianism, and violence rule? These are difficult questions at which this primer aims to only shed some initial light.

Muslims should note that the Prophet Muhammad (PBUH) was not a revolutionary who established a system from scratch but rather a social reformer. He did not invent any new commercial law or economic policy. Based on his divine guidance, however, he introduced measures that enabled a fair and just society to develop. He proscribed price control because from his own experience he knew that it was unfair to traders. When he introduced various options of use of land that had been conquered by the Muslims' army, he was creating choices for his community while also thinking for future generations. When he proscribed Muslims from taking others' property unlawfully, he reinforced an important principle of a fair society. When he forbade usury in lending, he was eliminating an instrument of economic exploitation of his time.

In the same spirit, the institutions proposed in this framework do not offer any grand projects. What they offer is a considered, evolving strategy. Let us recap the basic policy messages:

1. In Islam, private property rights enjoy sanctity, but there are limitations to these rights. In addition to the ethical constraints on buying and selling property, these limitations include payment of an annual wealth tax and compulsory distribution after death of the owner per the divine law.

2. Land and natural resources cannot be converted into private property but remain under public control, which can be managed by private parties against certain terms and conditions.

3. No price controls are needed, except in a public emergency or natural disaster. Prices will be set by market participants.

4. Deception, exploitation, or coercion in commercial transactions will not be tolerated, and an effective market regulatory mechanism should be in place.

5. The tax system will comprise of low and flat rates, following the *zakat* model.

6. Tariffs will be kept at a minimum rate to allow free flow of goods.

7. The authority of a central bank to print currency should be restricted by provision of an asset-backed arrangement to curtail fiat currency, with preference to a gold-backed system.

8. Financial institutions are allowed and licensed for all services other than charging any amount of interest on cash loans.

9. The government may facilitate and encourage voluntary institutions for social protection on the pattern of *waqf,* but they have no right to confiscate them. All *waqf* institutions or foundations should be "denationalized" and should be returned to their original private owners.

Most of these points can be used as broad policy direction. It follows that some institutions would have to be abolished. Many countries control prices, a practice that should stop, on condition that measures for consumer protection and fair trade have been put in place. Likewise, many existing laws and institutions would need to be reviewed.

For example, the legal treatment for ownership of natural resources would need to be reviewed and reformed, allowing for safeguards for private-sector investment. Similarly, private-sector investment in oil exploration depends on the probability of return on investment as well as on safety and security, and such would need to be incorporated in long-term contracts. Regarding land ownership, most countries have a legal frame-work to convert a private property into a public asset subject to fair compensation. Regarding public finance, this would be the most complex issue when tax collection would consist only of *zakat, ushr,* and land use tax. Can a state meet its needs if it has no other source? *Zakat,* however, might vary from 2.5 percent to 20 percent of income. And this is applied on both wealth *and* income. Regarding rural or urban infrastructure development, an additional land use tax can be imposed. But it should be recalled that the idea of low and restrictive taxes is by design—the role of government should be limited and its mandate constrained by its revenue.

Islamic teachings inspire many elected governments in Muslim-majority countries, and it is high time for them to consider applying these principles. In fact, any government, Muslim or non-Muslim, interested in an economic system based on freedom and fairness should examine these proposals. Were some non-Muslim states to take a lead in implementing these reforms, that would set a good example for others to follow.

Finally, it is worth emphasizing that the Islamic economic framework provides maximum liberty to economic life without obstructing a just order. In fact, for Islam, liberty is the essence of justice—and without liberty, a just God cannot hold His servants accountable.

Appendix 1

EVOLUTION OF ISLAMIC ECONOMICS

This primer has developed an Islamic case of economic liberty, citing primary sources of knowledge in Islam and thereby explaining what I have referred to as the Islamic economic framework.[1] As I earlier discussed, however, the model called "Islamic economics," which was developed in the mid-twentieth century by Muslims with collectivist leanings, does not endorse this case of economic liberty. This section explains how this literature of "Islamic economics" developed and argues why it is not consistent with the classical principles of economics in Islam.

At the start, I must highlight a point: current global debate on interlinks between "Islamic economics" is mostly influenced by modern-day writers, both from theological and social science backgrounds. Whenever a discussion takes place on the economic framework introduced by Islam, the reference points are

---

[1] This appendix is taken and adapted from some of my earlier work and was originally published in a slightly different form in *State Intervention in Commodity Markets: Discord between Economic Freedom and Social Justice in Islam* (Islamabad, Pakistan: Economic Freedom Network Pakistan/Friedrich-Naumann-Stiftung für die Freiheit, 2012), 25–35. Reprinted by permission of the author and the publisher.

mostly these twentieth-century writers. In contrast, little work has been done to introduce classical Islamic thoughts on matters of economic policy, as I have shown while discussing price control.

Iraqi cleric Muhammad Baqir al-Sadr (d. 1980) and Pakistani jurist Abu-'Ala Mawdudi (d. 1979) were the earliest proponents of "Islamic economics" as a distinct field. Mawdudi, who started writing about "Islamic economics" in the 1930s, criticized both capitalism as an economic system and Marxism as a godless view of society.

"Islamic economics" took about fifty years till it was finally recognized as an academic discipline in the First International Conference on Islamic Economics in Mecca in 1976.[2] The basic idea of "Islamic economics" is that it offers a distinctive economic framework based on the injunctions of Qur'an, Sunnah and Hadith. This framework, Islamic economists claim, is fundamentally different from the foundations of both capitalism and socialism. This also implies that "Islamic economics" must be recognized and organized as a social science—like economics itself. It ought to have its own methodological and epistemological framework.

IS ISLAMIC ECONOMY PLAN BASED OR MARKET BASED?

The modern discourse on "Islamic economics" is pregnant with an intellectual tension between economic freedom and social justice. This intellectual tension can be generalized by asking this

---

[2] Khurshid Ahmad, ed., *Studies in Islamic Economics: A Selection of Papers, Presented to the First International Conference on Islamic Economics Held at Makka under the Auspices of King Abdul Aziz University, Jeddah, February 21–26, 1976 (Ṣafar 21–26, 1396 H.)* (Jeddah, Saudi Arabia: International Centre for Research in Islamic Economics/King Abdul Aziz University; Leicester, UK: Islamic Foundation, 1980). For a list of participants and papers presented, see the conference program at the Islamic Economics Institute, https://iei.kau.edu.sa/Pages-E -ListConference1.aspx.

question: Is an Islamic economy market based or plan based, or a combination of the two approaches? The following section revisits the thoughts of modern Islamic economists, spanning about the past fifty years. As this discussion unfolds, the intellectual discord within Islamic thought seems to have been given up to intellectual reactions to history.

An early writer in the field of "Islamic economics," M. A. Mannan (b. 1938) perhaps captured the gist of his discipline in these words: "In an Islamic economy, the heart of the problem lies *not* in the prices offered by the market, but in the existing level of inequality of income."[3] This aptly reflects a tension between economic freedom and social justice, in which price would denote economic freedom, and income inequality would denote social justice. This may also be considered a touchstone of "Islamic economics." It has concerned itself with the causes of poverty instead of causes of prosperity. It discusses wealth redistribution more fondly than wealth creation. It is also an early signal that in the view of modern Islamic economists, *shari'ah* would prefer a plan-based economy and would focus on reducing income equalities.

Contrast this belief with a twentieth-century representative of classical Islamic legal thought, Ibn Ashur, who believed that "easing production and distribution of commodities is the most important objective of exchange in the *shari'ah*."[4]

Consider, for instance, Pakistani economist Syed Nawab Haider Naqvi, who has outlined a complete ethical Islamic

---

[3] Muhammad Abdul Mannan, *The Frontiers of Islamic Economics*, IAD Religio-Philosophy (Original) Series 13 (Delhi, India: Idarah-i Adabiyat-i Delli, 1984), 140, https://archive.org/details/frontiers ofislam0000mann.

[4] Quoted in Muhammad Lawal Ahmad Bashar, "Price Control in an Islamic Economy إسلامي اقتصاد في التسعير," *Journal of King Abdulaziz University: Islamic Economics* 9, no. 1 (1997): 40.

economy.[5] In such an economy, the framework will include the following requirements:

1. The level and composition of production and consumption will be under direct and indirect control of the Islamic society or state.

2. All citizens irrespective of their ability to earn will be guaranteed a reasonable level of income.

3. Feasible rates of growth will be subjected to an upper limit to "ensure a fair distribution of income and wealth now."

4. Income will be absolutely equalized.

5. The distribution of wealth will be equalized.

6. Exploitation will be minimized by "making labor's share a function of the total profits of the industry."

7. The institution of private property will be substantially diluted.

8. Enterprises will be taken over by the state.[6]

It is very tempting to call this framework an Islamic edition of *The Communist Manifesto*. It is because Naqvi has included production planning, consumption rationing, equality of income and wealth, erosion of private property, and shareholding labor as key elements of his own framework of Islamic economy. It seems that this thinking is a mirror reflection of the ideological clash between capitalism and communism, which marks one of the most important characteristics of the twentieth century. It is very difficult to trace any basis of these commandments within *shari'ah*. Calls for income equality and denial of private property are against widely accepted precepts of *shari'ah*.

---

[5] Syed Nawab Haider Naqvi, *Ethics and Economics: An Islamic Synthesis*, Islamic Economic Series 2 (Leicester, UK: Islamic Foundation, 1981).

[6] Naqvi, *Ethics and Economics*, 102f, 96, 65, 149, 64 (page numbers sequence by the author).

CAN THE MARKET BE HELD ACCOUNTABLE
FOR SOCIAL DISTRIBUTIVE JUSTICE?

The defenders of "Islamic economics" justify social distributive justice as a touchstone of economic policy. Just like secular socialists, these economists hold the market responsible for poverty and inequality. They view private ownership as exploitative in character. For a representation of this view, I have taken the example of a detailed article by Ahmad Hasan, who presents his views on social justice in Islam.[7]

Hasan relies on Imam al-Ghazali, the towering theologian of classic Islamic thought, for arguing his social justice theory. As quoted by Hasan, Al-Ghazali has defined five fundamental rights to everyone in the society—namely, protection of his religion, of his life, of his reason, of his posterity, and of his property.[8] Obviously, this list calls for essentially a protective policy, not a distributive policy, on the part of the state. We can understand this difference by invoking the concept of negative and positive freedoms as articulated by British philosopher and political theorist Isaiah Berlin (d. 1997).[9] Negative freedom implies freedom from coercion or constraints, especially when this coercion emanates from laws. Positive freedom means the ability to do something, to follow one's free will.

Imam al-Ghazali clearly advocated the notion of "negative freedom." But this is lost on Muslim socialists such as Ahmad Hasan. In fact, Hasan arm-twists the classification of al-Ghazali to argue that "the Qur'an insists on providing the basic necessities of life to all the members of the Muslim society."[10] For

---

[7] Ahmad Hasan, "Social Justice in Islam," *Islamic Studies* 10, no. 3 (1971): 209–19, https://www.jstor.org/stable/20833034.

[8] Hasan, "Social Justice in Islam," 211.

[9] Isaiah Berlin, *Two Concepts of Liberty: An Inaugural Lecture Delivered before the University of Oxford on 31 October 1958* (Oxford: Clarendon Press, 1958).

[10] Hasan, "Social Justice in Islam," 212.

the record, however, the Qur'anic text does not contain any such lists.

While Hasan may be regarded as an extreme example of an Islamic socialist writing in the heyday of communism, the concept of the role of justice in an economic policy also influences even those scholars who have otherwise established freedom of trade as an "over-riding factor of the *shari'ah*'s price control rulings."[11]

Consider this quote by the same author:

> Justice is the cardinal duty, indeed the raison d'être, of the (Islamic) not only in its retributive sense of adjudicating grievances but also in the government sense of *distributive justice, of establishing equilibrium of benefits and advantages in the community.*[12]

Another prominent Pakistani jurist, Imran Ahsan Khan Nyazee, maintains that "the real problem for the economic subsystem, and for "Islamic economics" as a discipline, is to identify in the light of the *maqasid* [higher goals or purposes] what kind of distributive justice is advocated by Islam."[13]

Kamali's distributive justice conflicts with the goals of retributive justice and begs this question: How can a system guaranteeing freedom of trade ensure "equilibrium of benefits and advantages"? Freedom ought to result into unequal benefits, and economic inequality is an accepted, taken-for-granted state in an Islamic economy. The essence of justice is not equality but freedom, as suggested by Ibn-e Khaldun:

---

[11] Kamali, *Maqasid al-Shari'ah Made Simple*. 26.

[12] Kamali, *Maqasid al-Shari'ah Made Simple*.

[13] Imran Ahsan Khan Nyazee, *Islamic Jurisprudence: Uṣ ūl al-Fiqh*, Islamic Law and Jurisprudence Series 3 (Islamabad, Pakistan: International Institute of Islamic Thought/Islamic Research Institute, 2000), 381.

Whoever takes someone's property, or uses him for forced labor, or presses an unjustified claim against him, or imposes upon him a duty not required by the religious law, does an *injustice* to that particular person ... It should be known that this is what the Lawgiver (Muhammad) actually had in mind when he forbade injustice.[14]

Expressing his views on market prices and equity, Mannan writes that "market prices may not enable all the potential consumers and producers to enter into the market."[15] He is right about this important assumption, but as a matter of fact, prices function as a means of expressing preference. As most Islamic economists do, Mannan also conflates the concept of freedom by confusing it with ability.[16] Freedom is essentially determined by absence of coercion, particularly coercion from a lawful authority but also from other humans. If a person lacks the ability or favorable circumstances to enter a market, then this is not due to coercion. Just as Ibn-e Khaldun elaborated, the spirit of justice is the absence of coercion.

It is not that all Islamic economists have expressed their reservations about the institution of the market. Consider these foundations of Islamic economy, elaborated by S. M. Yusuf: "(1) no

---

[14] Abd Ar Rahman bin Muhammed ibn Khaldun, *The Muqaddimah*, trans. Franz Rosenthal, accessed March 26, 2020, https://asadulla-hali.files.wordpress.com/2012/10/ibn_khaldun-al_muqaddimah.pdf, chapter 3, sec. 41.

[15] Mannan, *The Frontiers of Islamic Economics*, 136.

[16] Amartya Sen introduced this concept of freedom and capability in *Development as Freedom* (Oxford: Oxford University Press, 1999). He thinks that if a person is poor, then he is not free. In my opinion, he is mistaken, as I explain in the text. Freedom, or the lack of it, is largely an external phenomenon. When state and society impose certain conditions on our growth, they are reducing our freedom. But the mere fact that we are born poor does not make us unfree unless imposed from the outside.

corner market (i.e., no hoarding), (2) no hoarding of gold and silver, (3) no price control, (4) no restrictions in trade,[17] and (5) maintenance of a gold standard."[18] Yusuf's understanding of an Islamic economy is "negative" in character, a spirit much closer to the original, least-restrictive attitude toward the market. But a cursory comparison between the thoughts of modernists and classicist thinkers, and even traditionalists of the modern age, reveals that our traditionalist thinkers certainly expressed a more supportive attitude toward the market.

While it is understandable that equality of outcomes is not possible or desirable, we often call for equal opportunities. Provision of equal opportunities is a desirable goal but is impractical in a literal sense at a policy level. Even within a family, parents with all love and care for their children would know that their equal spending on their children's education will generate unequal results because of the differences in capacity, interest, and luck. More so, the government cannot ensure the provision of equal opportunities to all citizens in terms of education, health, and infrastructure; it can and should ensure the provision of minimum standards of public goods, however. Apart from a guarantee of minimum standards, the state must also ensure elimination of any legal and institutional discrimination against its citizens. A reasonable concept of equality, therefore, is based on these dual characteristics: no discrimination and provision of minimum standards of public goods. This can provide most citizens a reasonable opportunity to seek what is best for them.

---

[17] During this research, I have been struck by the evidence for freedom of trade during the Prophet's time, even with one's enemies (except arms and weapons).

[18] Yusuf, *Economic Justice in Islam*, 40.

Moral Engineering of the Individual: Predicament of Islamic Economics?

Muhammad Nejatullah Siddiqui (b. 1931) is one of the most important authorities on "Islamic economics" in the modern age. For him, "Islamic economics" questions some of the fundamental assumptions of modern economic theory, for instance, about human behavior. He believes that the stereotyping and universalization of human behavior, such as its risk aversion, is Western.[19] It is, for Siddiqi, this attitude toward risk that is described as a basic rationale of bank interest. Thus, in his view, "Islamic economics" is built on transformation of the individual's behavior.[20] Discussion of human behavior has emerged as a favorite topic of Islamic economists. They rightly know that without transformation of an individual into an Islamic person, free of selfishness, the dream of an Islamic economy, per their own ideals, will not mature. In other words, the Islamists envision nothing short of social engineering to purge impure human beings of their illicit desires.

Consider, for instance, another popular Islamic economist, M. Umer Chapra (b. 1933), who recognizes the efficiency of market strategy but believes that human beings are to be "reformed sufficiently."[21] But this construct takes a presumptuous approach toward the individual, which entails a possible predicament for Islamic economists: positing changed human behavior as a precondition for a utopian Islamic economy essentially means they are depending on external social factors to influence people's behavior. Thus the Islamic economists build the foundations

---

[19] Muhammad Nejatullah Siddiqi, *Economics: An Islamic Approach* (Islamabad, Pakistan: Institute of Policy Studies/Islamic Foundation, 2001), 61.

[20] Siddiqi, *Economics*, 61.

[21] M. Umer Chapra, *Islam and Economic Development*, Islamization of Knowledge 14 (Islamabad, Pakistan: International Institute of Islamic Thoughts/Islamic Research Institute, 1993), 127.

of "Islamic economics" on the assumption of specific human conduct instead of on certain methodologies and principles. Is it an escape?

Contemporary Lebanese academic Ayman Reda, while addressing the relationship between Islam and markets, has argued that "a significant part of the literature on Islam and markets has sought to examine this relationship from an initial assumption of mutual antagonism, or even incompatibility."[22] This approach, as Reda further argues, "has created a perceived conflict between Islam on one hand, and markets on the other."[23]

Muhammad Akram Khan, in his comprehensive critique of "Islamic economics," *What Is Wrong with Islamic Economics?*, argues that "most of what goes under the rubric of Islamic economics is a crude mimicry of conventional economics embellished with verses of the Qur'an and Traditions of the Prophet."[24] Khan believes that many Muslim economists draw inspiration from a romantic view of early-day Islamic society and paint a picture of a welfare state while ignoring the realities of Muslim societies today.[25]

Khan has proposed the term "Islamic economic teachings" instead of "Islamic economics,"[26] by which he implies that these teachings can supplement the human intellect and reasoning instead of replacing it. By giving one example, he mentions that while conventional economics talks about wealth creation and distribution, Islamic economic teachings can add spiritual and ethical dimensions. Khan concludes that "the Islamic economic system is a type of capitalism with a spiritual dimension."[27]

---

[22] Ayman Reda, "Islam and Markets," *Review of Social Economy* 71, no. 1 (2013): 20–43, https://doi.org/10.1080/00346764.2012.761752.

[23] Reda, "Islam and Markets," 20–43.

[24] Khan, *What Is Wrong with Islamic Economics?*, xv.

[25] Khan, *What Is Wrong with Islamic Economics?*, 20.

[26] Khan, *What Is Wrong with Islamic Economics?*, xv, 37, 49, 52, 57.

[27] Khan, *What Is Wrong with Islamic Economics?*, xv.

In another critical assessment of "Islamic economics," Malaysian sociologist Syed Farid Alatas concludes that as a subject, "Islamic economics" remains couched within the Western modernist discourse, is devoid of a political economy approach, and promises to study economic institutions from a moral point only.[28]

IS OUR MODERNITY REGRESSIVE?

Overall, the tradition of Islamic jurisprudence, and in particular its verdicts on economic policy, has endorsed a market-friendly, liberal, and limited government philosophy. Though, as I noted in the earlier section, subtle and important differences do remain in various schools of thought. If the jurists stood, generally, for economic freedom, in what ways have distributive tendencies crept into the thought of modern Islamic economists?

I argue that the classical jurists of Islam are separated from their modern counterparts by a sharp historical wedge that is known as colonization. The rise of "Islamic economics" on the backdrop of resurgence in the Islamization of knowledge is essentially a twentieth-century phenomenon that draws its parallel with the independence of most Muslim countries or their defeat at the hands of Western powers. Thus, Islamic economists of all varieties are asserting a reaction. That leads to the creation of novelties such as Islamic socialism or Islamic capitalism wherein the economic exegesis of classical Muslim jurists is free from any such epistemological apologies. That is why it is important for us to rediscover the economic insights offered in earlier texts, not in search of some sort of a puritan brand of economic system, for no such system exists or is desirable. Rather, this discovery should be inspired to get only

---

[28] Syed Farid Alatas, "Islam and the Science of Economics," in *The Blackwell Companion to Contemporary Islamic Thought*, ed. Ibrahim M Abu-Rabi', Blackwell Companions to Religion (Oxford: Blackwell, 2006), 587–606.

historical understanding of certain developments, particularly those intellectual manifestations that draw authority from the religion and continue to influence the domain of public policy in Islamic countries. In countries like Pakistan, where the constitution is officially subject to the boundaries defined by *shari'ah*, such analysis gains even more importance.

As my analysis of price freedom has hopefully shown, the spirit of economic policy in view of *shari'ah* was noninterventionist and nondistributive in character. It looked at the market participants and especially traders as "do-gooders" and defined legal restrictions for the state, discouraging its intervention in the markets.

There is no doubt that Islam calls for compassion for others. But the calls for brotherhood were essentially moral and voluntary in nature; otherwise, the example of *mu'akhat* (brotherhood) set by the Prophet and his worthy companions on *hijra*, wherein the Muslims of Medina shared and gave up half their properties to their migrated brethren from Mecca, would have been codified into a law. Such a law would have held that any surplus property owned by a Muslim should be given up to a needy brother. Thus, this brotherhood remains voluntary in nature and not legally enforceable. The appropriation of one's property is considered, by consensus, an injustice (*zulm*). Mere acquisition and possession of property does not draw any sanction. Thus, the concept of a forced redistribution seems alien to Islamic law and the spirit of its injunctions.

As discussed earlier concerning wealth creation,[29] the Qur'anic vision of economic transactions is based on the fundamental principle of voluntary exchange and thriftiness:

> Believers, do not consume your wealth among yourselves in vanity, but rather trade with it by mutual consent. (Qur'an 4:29)

---

[29] See discussion under sec. 2.2, "Wealth Creation."

The Qur'an has made it categorically clear that what individuals get will be either out of their effort or their God's bounty—that is, His *fadl*, a favor without necessarily deserving one. The Qur'an says, "That man can have nothing but that he strives for" (53:39). And at many times, it mentions the Lord's bounty as a favor from Him. For instance, the Qur'an elsewhere says, "That Allah may reward them [according to] the best of what they did and increase them from His bounty. And Allah gives provision to whom He wills without account" (24:38). It seems that just as our faith moves like a pendulum between "fear and hope," in the words of Qur'an, our sustenance, our economic results also oscillate between our efforts and our luck.[30]

ECONOMIC FREEDOM WARRANTS SOCIAL JUSTICE

We have addressed the intellectual discord between economic freedom and social justice at two levels: one is at the general, conceptual level, and the second is at the specific, applicational level in the case of proscribing price control. Relying almost entirely on the primary and secondary sources of Islamic law, Islamic philosophy, and "Islamic economics" within the Islamic world, one can argue that while *shari'ah* calls for establishing an order of economic freedom based on fair competition and stringent consumer protection measures, the modern discipline of "Islamic economics" seems to have drifted away in an opposite direction. Barring a few dissenting voices, the mainstream thought in "Islamic economics" prefers to discuss poverty instead of wealth creation, income variations rather than prices, and the role of the state rather than the role of the market. "Islamic economics" is also built on the assumption of an imaginary, utopian "Islamic individual" whose incentives are supposedly different from ordinary human beings. This literature has essentially developed a system that provides spiritual justification of both market-based and plan-based economies

---

[30] Qur'an, 32:16.

without necessarily taking a clear position on the principles, methodology, and legal framework. The general tone of modern "Islamic economics," however, remains statist and redistributive.

The intellectual discord between economic freedom and social justice within classical Islamic thought has seemingly been replaced by a historical wedge between a medieval, market-centric thought and a modern, statist ideology.

One should never forget Islam was introduced by a Prophet who led the active life of a merchant for twenty long years and who attributed every nine out of ten sources of sustenance and provision to trade. This is only possible if the economic organization is enterprise-centric instead of state-centric. The letter of *shari'ah* guarantees economic freedom, and its spirit enjoins social justice. The spirit of welfare, which Islam propagates, is based on the degree of choice and freedom that an individual has and is dependent on the absence of coercion. Such welfare does not come from a big state; it comes from prosperous and responsible individuals who imbibe the notion of mutual goodwill.

Appendix 2

ISLAM AND CAPITALISM— MAWDUDI REVISITED

The majority of scholars writing on Islam and economics have taken a position that Islam offers a middle path between two "extremes"—that is, between capitalism, which is built on private property; and socialism, which is built on absolute negation of private property. This position has almost reached a consensus level now at which both traditional scholars and trained economists largely agree. The voices promoting "Islamic socialism" and "Islamic capitalism" are few. On the balance, however, we find that price freedom, property rights, and low taxes find greater mention (and objection) in the debate on "Islamic economics" than central planning and income equality. This preference is not without deep misconceptions about capitalism itself. Hence, one needs to address the understanding of free-market capitalism that has permeated "Islamic economics."

Debate over "Islamic economics" has advanced considerably since the time of Sayyid Abu-'Ala Mawdudi (d. 1979), the founder of Jamaat-e-Islami of Pakistan and a prolific and popular writer who was not only one of the pioneering proponents of "Islamic economics" but also of the broader notion of "political Islam," or Islamism. But the main arguments that he presented are still in vogue. After Mawdudi first introduced "Islamic economics" eighty years ago, this subject has been included in more than a hundred universities in the world. In his home country of Pakistan, Islamization of education, politics, the constitution, and to some degree the economy are largely attributable to Maulana Mawdudi.

Mawdudi published extensively on topics such as private property, interest, and land reforms in the 1940s and 1950s. His writings were presented in *Ma'āshiyyāt-i Islām* in a single Urdu volume first published in 1969, which was translated into English as *First Principles of Islamic Economics* and published after the 2008 Global Financial Crisis.[1] In the foreword, Khurshid Ahmad, an eminent Islamic economist in his own right, compares Mawdudi with both Adam Smith and Karl Marx, arguing that both these intellectual giants were not economists per se.[2] Consequently, Mawdudi, in this view, is the key founder of "Islamic economics." So we need to revisit his views.

We will not discuss Mawdudi's analysis of specific issues such as land reforms, usury, and *zakat*. But it is worthwhile to understand the perspective of Mawdudi on capitalism itself. In chapter 3 of his work *First Principles of Islamic Economics*, "The Differences between Islam and Capitalism," Mawdudi, like almost all Islamic economists after him, stresses that wealth must *not* be allowed to accumulate. He writes that "to amass savings and then use them to produce more wealth is the basis

---

[1] For the publication history of this work, see the bibliography. See also related note in the foreword.

[2] Adam Smith (d. 1790) was a Scottish philosopher often identified as the father of modern capitalism who is best known for his *Inquiry into the Nature and Causes of the Wealth of Nations* (1776). Karl Marx (d. 1883) was a German philosopher and socialist revolutionary who is best known for coauthoring the 1848 pamphlet *Manifest der Kommunistichen Partei* (*Manifesto of the Communist Party*) and the three-volume *Das Kapital: Kritik der politischen Okonomie* (*Capital: A Critique of Political Economy*; 1867, 1885, 1894).

of capitalism"[3] and presents this as something inherently corrupt. He insists that instead of being accumulated, money has to be spent. "Islam's approach totally differs from that of capitalism," he argues. "A capitalist thinks that he would go bankrupt by spending, but become wealthier by stockpiling his riches" (68). He claims that "instead of going waste, wealth actually rises by spending and ... interest causes greater loss rather than helping our amount to multiply" (70). So he proposes what he considers to be "an absolutely new theory" that is "diametrically opposed to the capitalist viewpoint" (70).

Mawdudi then mentions *zakat*, which is the obligatory annual deduction from a Muslim's wealth beyond a certain threshold level. He writes that "Islam and capitalism stand in sharp contrast to each other" and argues that capitalism demands that money be saved and invested, whereas Islam enjoins free flow of capital. "In the capitalist system, the exchange of wealth is restrained, while in Islam it is unchecked" (75). To materialize this unchecked flow of capital, he suggests that "those in possession of wealth should deposit their wealth (resources) in excess of their requirements in a reservoir, and those in need should come forward and fill their buckets" (75). He doesn't answer questions such as if some people can "fill their buckets" freely, why would they ever work? And why would this not amount to anything other than the exploitation of the people who do work and create wealth?

Mawdudi also presents a list of moral principles and regulations that are "basic ingredients and mainstays" of the Islamic economic system (61). Foremost is the "distinction between lawful [*halal*] and forbidden [*haram*] means of livelihood," as "Islam does not give free license to its followers to earn a living or to conduct their economic activities as they choose" (61). Under the forbidden activities, Mawdudi includes bribery, embezzlement, breach of trust, theft, mishandling of orphans' property, fraudulent transactions, sex trade, obscenity, alcoholic

---

[3] Mawdudi, *First Principles of Islamic Economics*, 67.

beverages, gambling, betting, trading in idols, and usury (63–66). His other points refer to the law of inheritance, war gains, revenue distribution, and finally, injunctions about economy and balance, which I will not discuss in detail.

Mawdudi's critique of capitalism can be paraphrased as follows: Capitalism is an economic system that is essentially based on savings, which leads to investment and hence more capital accumulation, while interest functions as a critical tool in this process. This inevitably leads to concentration of wealth in fewer hands, which results in inequalities and injustices. Mawdudi's interpretation of Islamic principles of economic organization, apart from moral injunctions with which we will not disagree, rests on the singular idea of wealth circulation, for which his policy tool is *zakat*. At the risk of oversimplifying, I can say that Mawdudi equated capitalism with wealth concentration, and "Islamic economics" with wealth circulation. In both cases, he misses one important question: how wealth is created. Given Mawdudi's influence in this field, it is no coincidence, then, that we find this question largely missing from "Islamic economics."

In modern times we find an echo of this savings-led capital stock accumulation theory in Thomas Piketty's highly acclaimed book *Capital in the Twenty-first Century*.[4] Based on his review of historical data, Piketty arrives at the same conclusion: the owners of capital have been able to accumulate wealth at a faster speed than the general economic growth, causing huge imbalances in the wealth ownership both within and between economies. Piketty's methodology has been now challenged, however, causing doubts about his conclusions, which pertain to how he estimates the capital/income ratio, an overestimate of returns of capital without considering inflation, and a static view of class differences in a society.

---

[4] Thomas Piketty, *Capital in the Twenty-First Century*, trans. Arthur Goldhammer (Cambridge, MA: Belknap Press of Harvard University Press, 2014).

There are several problems with Mawdudi's interpretation of capitalism as well as his interpretation of Islam. As will be obvious to many, wealth creation cannot be narrowly defined as a process of savings and investment. In fact, this seems to be a very neoclassical model, and Mawdudi may have been influenced by the writings of British economist John Maynard Keynes. At best, savings is a necessary but not a sufficient condition for wealth accumulation—which is as true in the life of an individual as in the life of a nation. Under normal circumstances, open trade, competition, and entrepreneurship provide unlimited opportunities to bearers of fresh ideas to start new businesses and accumulate wealth. Mawdudi does not discuss the role of innovation in economic growth, as he does not consider it central to the process of wealth creation.

Early Islamic history presents several inspiring examples of how the companions of the Prophet, who as I have noted was himself a successful merchant, accumulated huge capital while literally starting from a rag. One famous example is Abdul Rehman bin Auf, who led a caravan of seven hundred camels within years of migration to Medina. There is a great wisdom in the hadith that declares:

> An honest and trustworthy merchant will be [raised] with the Prophets, the truthful and the martyrs. (Al-Tirmidhi, hadith no. 1209)[5]

An honest merchant, for Islam, is as important as a prophet, and capitalism provides necessary conditions for merchants to thrive.

---

[5] Al-Tirmidhi, *Jami' at-Tirmidhi*, The Book on Business, accessed on March 22, 2020, https://sunnah.com/tirmidhi/14. This hadith is considered *daif* (weak in terms of authenticity).

GHAMIDI: RELIGIOUS CASE
FOR A LIMITED GOVERNMENT

In many ways, Javed Ahmad Ghamidi is an antithesis of Maulana Mawdudi. Born in Punjab, Pakistan, Ghamidi is a traditional scholar of Islam who received his initial education from Mawdudi himself and was once considered protégé to Mawdudi at the young age of twenty-two, until he was expelled from Jamaat-e-Islami after voicing differences of opinion with Mawdudi's understanding of Islam. By the late 1970s, Ghamidi began to show a different approach to interpreting the Qur'an, closely following his second mentor, Amin Ahsan Islahi (d. 1997), himself a notable scholar and author of *Tadabbur-i-Qur'an*, a *tafsir* (exegesis or commentary) of the Qur'an.[6] Ghamidi today represents the same intellectual tradition and established his own institute, Al-Mawrid, in Lahore, Pakistan,[7] attracting several young researchers from modern disciplines who have devoted themselves to learning his ideas. He is a popular scholar of Islam in the conservative nation of Pakistan and in the Urdu-speaking Muslim community worldwide, with largely an urban following. In 2008, Ghamidi had to leave the country fearing execution from the Taliban as he became vocal on the issue of jihad, which he considers legitimate only if an Islamic government were to lead it. He spent the next nine years in Malaysia, where he continued publishing and educating his followers using modern means of communication and occasional travels. In 2018, Ghamidi moved to the United States, where he is now based.[8] Not surprisingly, Ghamidi also has his share of detrac-

---

[6] Amin Ahsan Islahi, *Tadabbur-e-Qur'ān: Pondering over the Qur'ān*, trans. Mohammad Saleem Kayani, 2 vols. (Kuala Lumpur, Malaysia: Islamic Book Trust, 2006–). See bibliography for the original nine-volume series in Urdu.

[7] For more on Al-Mawrid, a foundation for Islamic research and education, see http://www.al-mawrid.org/.

[8] For more on Javed Ahmad Ghamidi, see https://www.javedahmedghamidi.org/.

tors, mostly coming from traditional theologians. Ghamidi draws intellectual inspiration for his theological work from Allama Muhammad Iqbal (d. 1938), who wrote a pathbreaking book, *Reconstruction of Religious Thought in Islam.*[9] Ghamidi's project is nothing short of a bold and rational reconstruction of *shari'ah* while confining it to the bounds of the primary sources of knowledge in Islam.

One of the fundamental points of departure from Mawdudi's school of thought is that Ghamidi does not consider establishment of an Islamic state a religious obligation—which is the raison d'être of modern political Islam movements. He believes that the state of Medina was a natural social evolution, and the Prophet Muhammad set examples of conduct as a ruler, though we need to separate his worldly commandments from his religious mission. If this antithesis is accepted, the whole edifice of political Islam crumbles down.

In regard to the economy, Ghamidi believes that "the economic shari'ah has been revealed by the Almighty through His last Prophet (PBUH) for the purification of the economy and economic affairs of a country. It is based on the Qur'anic philosophy of creation."[10] Expounding this philosophy of creation, Ghamidi explains that "the Almighty has created this world as a trial and test for man; every person has therefore been made to depend on others for his living." This is because "the Almighty has blessed people with varying abilities, intelligence and inclinations as well as with varying means and resources. In fact, it is because of this variation that a society comes into being."[11]

Ghamidi invokes the following Qur'anic verse to substantiate his interpretation:

---

[9] Sir Muhammad Iqbal, *Six Lectures on the Reconstruction of Religious Thought in Islam* (Lahore, Pakistan: Kapur Art Printing Works, 1930).

[10] Ghamidi, *Islam,* 466–67.

[11] Ghamidi, *Islam,* 467.

Is it they who apportion your Lord's blessings? It is we
who deal out to them their livelihood in this world,
exalting some in rank above others, so that the one
may take the other into his service. Better is your Lord's
mercy than all their hoarded treasures. (43:32)

This is a religious case of comparative advantage and voluntary
exchange so that they can mutually serve each other.

In his explanation of the economic framework of *shari'ah*,
which Ghamidi refers to as "economic *shari'ah*," he lays emphasis
on *zakat* being the only legitimate tax that an Islamic government can impose.[12] As I discussed earlier concerning *zakat*,[13]
Ghamidi has an expansive interpretation of *zakat*, encompassing
all professions as sources for *zakat* collection and all possible
public expenditures as *zakat* expenditures. He makes a rather
provocative point. Besides *zakat*, tax is the modern form of
slavery, and while humankind has mostly gotten rid of slavery,
it still exists in the form of tax.[14] That is why the Almighty has
taken away the power of taxation from the government. At the
given rates of *zakat*, the powers and scope of such a government—which is financed only through *zakat* (barring other
nontax sources)—will be inevitably limited. This is, we can say,
the Islamic case for a limited government.

Ghamidi's understanding of "economic *shari'ah*" is very close
to the basic tenets of economic freedom—namely, limited
government and voluntary exchange, though he does not use
these terms. He strictly speaks from an Islamic theological
perspective and does not engage with the framework of the
social sciences, though he encourages his followers to apply

---

[12] Javed Ahmad Ghamidi, personal communication with author,
August 27, 2018.

[13] For the earlier discussion on *zakat* (obligatory tithe), see sec. 3.6,
"Islamic Fiscal Policy: Low and Flat Taxes."

[14] Javed Ahmad Ghamidi, personal communication with author,
August 27, 2018.

his religious thoughts in other fields. Therefore, in his own vocabulary, one cannot find the phrases that would be familiar to a nonreligious audience. He shows how and why Islam can promote a moral vision of the economy based on free markets and a limited state.

And Allah knows best.

BIBLIOGRAPHY

Abdullah, Adam et al. *Islamic Economics: Principles and Analysis*. Edited by Moutaz Abojeib, Mohamed Aslam Mohamed Haneef, and Mustafa Omar Mohammed. Kuala Lumpur, Malaysia: International Shari'ah Research Academy for Islamic Finance (ISRA)/Lorong University A, 2018.

Abu Dawud Sulayman ibn al-Ash'ath as-Sijistani. *Sunan Abī Dāwūd.* https://sunnah.com/abudawud.

———. *Sunan Abī Dāwūd* [in Arabic]. Edited by Shuʻayb Arnāʼūṭ and Muḥammad Kāmil Qarah Balilī. 7 vols. Beirut: Dār al-Risālah al-ʻĀlamīyah, 2009.

Abu Yusuf, Yakub ibn Ibrahim al-Ansari. *Kitab-ul-Kharaj.* Translated by Nejatullah Siddiqi. n.p.: n.p., n.d.

———. *Kitab al-Kharaj* (Book of taxation) [in Arabic]. Damascus, 1732. https://www.wdl.org/en/item/11225/.

Ahmad, Khurshid, ed. *Studies in Islamic Economics: A Selection of Papers, Presented to the First International Conference on Islamic Economics Held at Makka under the Auspices of King Abdul Aziz University, Jeddah, February 21–26, 1976 (Ṣafar 21–26, 1396 H.).* Jeddah, Saudi Arabia: International Centre for Research in Islamic Economics/King Abdul Aziz University; Leicester, UK: Islamic Foundation, 1980.

Alatas, Syed Farid. "Islam and the Science of Economics." Chap. 33 in *The Blackwell Companion to Contemporary Islamic Thought*, edited by Ibrahim M Abu-Rabi'. Blackwell Companions to Religion. Oxford: Blackwell, 2006.

Ali, Abdullah Yusuf. *Modern English Translation of the Holy Qur'an: Meanings and Commentary*. Jeddah: Dar al-Qiblah Co. for Islamic Literature, 1998.

Askari, Hossein, Zamir Iqbal, and Abbas Mirakhor. *Introduction to Islamic Economics: Theory and Application*. Wiley Finance. Hoboken, NJ: Wiley & Sons, 2015.

Baker, William W. *Endless Money: The Moral Hazards of Socialism*. Hoboken, NJ: Wiley & Sons, 2010.

Bashar, Muhammad Lawal Ahmad. "Price Control in an Islamic Economy التسعير في اقتصاد إسلامي." *Journal of King Abdulaziz University: Islamic Economics* 9, no. 1 (1997): 29–52.

Berg, Chris, and Andrew Kemp. "Islam's Free Market Heritage." *Institute of Public Affairs Review* 59, no. 1 (2007): 11–15.

Berlin, Isaiah. *Two Concepts of Liberty: An Inaugural Lecture Delivered before the University of Oxford on 31 October 1958*. Oxford: Clarendon Press, 1958.

al-Bukhari, Imam Muhammad. *Sahih al-Bukhari*. https://sunnah.com/bukhari.

———. *Sahih Al-Bukhari*. Beirut: Dar Ibn Kathir, 2002.

al-Butibi, Muhammad Amno. "Al-Maqbul Wa al-Mardud Min Tatabbu'i al-Rukhas Wa al-Talfiq Bayna al-Madhahib" (in Arabic). *Majallah Al-Madhhab al-Maliki*, 2006, 61–103.

Chapra, M. Umer. *Islam and Economic Development*. Islamization of Knowledge 14. Islamabad, Pakistan: International Institute of Islamic Thoughts/Islamic Research Institute, 1993. https://benrafick.files.wordpress.com/2009/12/islam-and-economic-development.pdf.

Dawood, N. J., trans. *The Koran*. 5th rev. ed. Penguin Classics. London: Penguin Books, 1999.

Furqani, Hafas. "Theory of Distributive Justice in Islamic Perspective: A Conceptual Exploration." Paper presented at the 6th International Conference on Islam and Liberty: Building an Islamic Case for Open Markets, Islamabad, Pakistan, November 15, 2018. Islam and Liberty Network. https://islamandlibertynetwork.org/blog/2018/12/30/hafas6/.

Gamal, Mahmoud A. el-. *Islamic Finance: Law, Economics, and Practice.* Cambridge: Cambridge University Press, 2006.

Ghamidi, Javed Ahmad. *Islam: A Comprehensive Introduction* (an English rendering of *Mizan*; citations in Arabic). Translated by Shehzad Saleem. Lahore, Pakistan: Al-Mawrid, 2010. https://www.javedahmedghamidi.org/#!/mizan. Digital copy also available at http://muqweb.yolasite.com/resources/Islam%20A%20comprehensive%20introduction%20-%20Javaid%20Ahmed%20Ghamidi.pdf

———. *Mīzān* (in Urdu). Lahore, Pakistan: Al-Mawrid, 2008. https://www.javedahmedghamidi.org/#!/mizan. Ghazanfar, S. M., ed. *Medieval Islamic Economic Thought: Filling the Great Gap in European Economics.* London: Taylor & Francis Books, 2003. https://doi.org/10.4324/9780203633700.

Haneef, Muhammad Aslam, and Emad Rafiq Barakat. "Must Money Be Limited to Only Gold and Silver? A Survey of Fiqhi Opinions and Some Implications." *Journal of King Abdulaziz University–Islamic Economics* 19, no. 1 (2006): 21–35.

Hasan, Ahmad. "Social Justice in Islam." *Islamic Studies* 10, no. 3 (1971): 209–19. https://www.jstor.org/stable/20833034.

Hasan-uz-Zaman, S. M. *Economic Functions of an Islamic State (The Early Experience).* Rev. ed. Islamic Economic Series 14. Karachi, Pakistan: Islamic Foundation, 1991.

Ibn Hajar al-Asqalani. *Bulugh al-Maram.* https://sunnah.com/bulugh.

Ibn Kathir. *Tafsir al-Qur'an al-'Azim.* Beirut: Mu'assassah al-Kutub al-Thaqafiyyah, 1996.

Ibn Khaldun, Abd Ar Rahman bin Muhammed. *The Muqaddimah.* Translated by Franz Rosenthal. Accessed March 26, 2020. https://asadullahali.files.wordpress.com/2012/10/ibn_khaldun-al_muqaddimah.pdf.

Ibn Majah al-Qazwini, Imam Muhammad bin Yazid. *Sunan Ibn Majah.* https://sunnah.com/ibnmajah.

Iqbal, Sir Muhammad. *Six Lectures on the Reconstruction of Religious Thought in Islam.* Lahore, Pakistan: Kapur Art Printing Works, 1930.

Islahi, Abdul Azim. "An Analytical Study of al-Ghazali's Thought on Money and Interest." Accessed November 20, 2019. https://mpra.ub.uni-muenchen.de/41438/.

———. *Economic Concepts of Ibn Taimīyah.* Islamic Economics Series 12. Leicester, UK: Islamic Foundation, 1988. https://archive.org/details/EconomicConceptsOfIbnTaymiyyah.

———. *Tadabbur-e-Qur'ān: Pondering over the Qur'ān.* Translated by Mohammad Saleem Kayani. 2 vols. Kuala Lumpur, Malaysia: Islamic Book Trust, 2006–. Originally published as *Tadabbur-i Qur'ān* [in Urdu]. 9 vols. Silsilah-i maṭbū'āt 1–9. Lahore, Pakistan: Fārān Fa'ūnḍeshan, 2006. http://www.tadabbur-i-quran.org/.

Islam, Md. Thowhidul. "Historical Development of Waqf Governance in Bangladesh: Challenges and Prospects." In *Building an Islamic Case for Open Markets,* edited by Ali Salman and Husnul Amin, 307–56. Islamabad, Pakistan: IRD, 2019.

Jaffar, Syammon, Adam Abdullah, and Ahamed Kameel Mydin Meera. "Fiat Money: From the Current Islamic Finance Scholars' Perspective." *Humanomics* 33, no. 3 (August 14, 2017): 274–99.

Kamali, Mohammad Hashim. *Maqāṣid Al-Sharī'ah Made Simple.* Occasional Papers Series 13. London: International Institute of Islamic Thought, 2008. https://doi.org/10.2307/j.ctvkc67vz.

———. *The Right to Life, Security, Privacy and Ownership in Islam.* Kuala Lumpur: International Institute of Advanced Islamic Studies Malaysia; Petaling Jaya, Malaysia: Ilmiah Publishers, 2013. First published 2007 in the series Fundamental Rights and Liberties in Islam 5 by Islamic Texts Society (Cambridge). Citations refer to the 2013 edition.

Khan, Muhammad Akram. *What Is Wrong with Islamic Economics?: Analysing the Present State and Future Agenda.* Studies in Islamic Finance, Accounting and Governance. Cheltenham, UK: Edward Elgar, 2013.

Khan, Muhammad Moinuddin, and M. H. Syed, eds. *Business and Trade in Islam.* Vol. 2 of *Encyclopaedia of Islamic Economy.* 5 vols. New Delhi, India: Pentagon Press, 2009.

Koehler, Benedikt. *Early Islam and the Birth of Capitalism.* Lanham, MD: Lexington Books, 2014.

———. "The Economist Mohammed Ibn Abdullah (570–632)." *Economic Affairs* 31, no. 1 (2011): 109–11.

Kuran, Timur. "Zakat: Islam's Missed Opportunity to Limit Predatory Taxation." SSRN Scholarly Paper. Economic Research Initiatives at Duke (ERID) Working Paper No. 284. Rochester, NY: Social Science Research Network, April 8, 2019. https://dx.doi.org/10.2139/ssrn.3368292.

Lemieux, Pierre. "Land Taxes: The Return of Henry George." Accessed March 25, 2020. The Library of Economics and Liberty. https://www.econlib.org/land-taxes-the-return-of-henry-george/.

Malik, Maszlee. "Welfare beyond the State: 'Ihsani' Societal-Based Welfare." In *Islamic Foundations of a Free Society,* edited by Nouh El Harmouzi and Linda Whetstone, 58–73. Hobart Paper 183. London: Institute of Economic Affairs, 2016. https://iea.org.uk/wp-content/uploads/2016/10/Islamic-Foundations-of-a-Free-Society.pdf.

Mannan, Muhammad Abdul. *The Frontiers of Islamic Economics.* IAD Religio-Philosophy (Original) Series 13. Delhi, India: Idarah-i Adabiyat-i Delli, 1984. https://archive.org/details/frontiersofislam0000mann.

Marx, Karl, and Friedrich Engels. *Das Kapital: Kritik der politischen Okonomie* [in German]. 3 vols. Hamburg: Meissner, 1867, 1885, 1894.

———. *Manifest der Kommunistichen Partei* [in German]. London: Gedruckt in der Office der Bildings-Gesellschaft fur Arbeiter von J. C. Burghard, 1848.

————. "Manifesto of the Communist Party" (1848). In *Karl Marx and Frederick Engels: Selected Works in Three Volumes,* translated by Samuel Moore in cooperation with rederick Engels, 1888, 1:98–137. Moscow: Progress Publishers, 1969. https://www.marxists.org/ archive/marx/works/download/pdf/Manifesto.pdf.

Masud, Muhammad Khalid. *Shari'a Today: Essays on Contemporary Issues and Debates in Muslim Societies.* IRD Series on Studies in Contemporary Islamic Thought 2. Islamabad, Pakistan: National Book Foundation/Iqbal International Institute for Research and Dialogue, 2013.

Mawdudi, Sayyid Abul A'la. *First Principles of Islamic Economics.* Edited by Khurshid Ahmad. Translated by Ahmad Imam Shafaq Hashemi. Markfield, UK: Islamic Foundation, 2011. Originally published as *Maʿāshiyyāt-i Islām* [in Urdu, with text-words in English and quotations and bibliographical references in Arabic]. Edited by Khurshid Ahmad. (Lahore, Pakistan: Islāmik Pablīkeshanz, 1969).

Mohammed, Naveed. "Al Azhar University Fatwa Allows for Fixed Returns on Bank Deposits." Islamic Finance Foundation/ Sukuk.com (website). March 20, 2014. https://www.sukuk.com/ education/al-azhar-university-fatwa-interest-bank-deposits-271/.

al-Munajjid, Muhammad Saalih. "What Is the Difference between Zakaah and Taxes, and Is It Permissible to Impose Taxes? Is It Obligatory to Pay Them?" Islam Question & Answer (website). September 30, 2013. https://islamqa.info/en/answers/130920/ the-difference-between-zakaah-and-taxes-and-the-conditions-of -imposing-taxes.

Naqvi, Syed Nawab Haider. *Ethics and Economics: An Islamic Synthesis.* Islamic Economic Series 2. Leicester, UK: Islamic Foundation, 1981.

al-Nawwawi, Yahya b. Sharaf. *Sharh Sahih Muslim.* Beirut: Dar al-Fikr, 1995.

Nezhad, Mansour Zarra. "A Brief History of Money in Islam and Estimating the Value of Dirham and Dīnār." *Review of Islamic Economics* 8, no. 2 (2004): 51–66.

al-Nisaburi, Muslim b. al-Hajjaj. *Sahih Muslim.* Riyadh: Dar Taybah, 2006.

Nyazee, Imran Ahsan Khan. *Islamic Jurisprudence: Uṣūl al-Fiqh.* Islamic Law and Jurisprudence Series 3. Islamabad, Pakistan: International Institute of Islamic Thought/Islamic Research Institute, 2000.

————. *The Prohibition of Riba Elaborated.* Islamic Banking Series 1. Islamabad, Pakistan: Advanced Legal Studies Institute, 2009.

Oguz, Orhan, and Ahmed Tabakoglu. "An Historical Approach to Islamic Pricing Policy: A Research on the Ottoman Price System and Its Application منهج تاريخي لبحث سياسة سعرية إسلامية بحث في نظام الأسعار في الدولة العثمانية وتطبيقاته." *Journal of King Abdulaziz University: Islamic Economics* 3, no. 1 (1991): 63–79.

Oran, Ahmad. "An Islamic Socio-Economic Public Interest Theory of Market Regulation." *Review of Islamic Economics* 14, no. 1 (January 1, 2010): 125–46.

O'Sullivan, Michael. "Interest, Usury, and the Transition from 'Muslim' to 'Islamic' Banks, 1908–1958." *International Journal of Middle East Studies* 52 (2020): 261–287. https://doi.org/10.1017/S0020743820000239.

Piketty, Thomas. *Capital in the Twenty-First Century.* Translated by Arthur Goldhammer. Cambridge, MA: Belknap Press of Harvard University Press, 2014. Originally published as *Le capital au XXIe siècle* (Paris: Éditions du Seuil, 2013).

al-Qazwini, Muhammad b. Yazid. *Sunan Ibn Majah.* Cairo: Matba'ah Dar Ihya' al-Kutub al 'Arabiyyah, M.F.A. Al-Baqi edition.

Rab, Hifzur. *Economic Justice in Islam: Monetary Justice and the Way Out of Interest (Riba).* Kuala Lumpur, Malaysia: Noordeen, 2006.

Rahman, Fazlur. "Ribā and Interest." *Islamic Studies* 3, no. 1 (March 1964): 1–43. www.jstor.org/stable/20832724.

Rauf, Imam Feisal Abdul. *Defining Islamic Statehood: Measuring and Indexing Contemporary Muslim States.* London: Palgrave Macmillan UK, 2015. https://doi.org/10.1057/9781137446824.

Rawls, John. *A Theory of Justice.* Cambridge, MA: Belknap Press of Harvard University Press, 1971.

Reda, Ayman. "Islam and Markets." *Review of Social Economy* 71, no. 1 (2013): 20–43. https://doi.org/10.1080/00346764.2012.761752.

al-Sakandari, Ahmad b. 'Ata Allah. *Al-Hikam Al-'Ata'Iyyah.* Damascus: Hasan Al-Samahi Suwaydan, 1997.

Salman, Ali. "The Libertarian Character of the Islamic Economy." *Economic Affairs* 33, issue 1 (2013): 108–118. https://doi.org/10.1111/ecaf.12003.

———. *State Intervention in Commodity Market: Discord between Economic Freedom and Social Justice in Islam.* Islamabad, Pakistan: Economic Freedom Network Pakistan/Friedrich-Naumann-Stiftung für die Freiheit, 2012.

Salman, Ali, and Husnul Amin, eds. *Building an Islamic Case for Open Markets.* Islamabad, Pakistan: IRD, 2019.

Sen, Amartya. *Development as Freedom.* Oxford: Oxford University Press, 1999.

Shirazi, Nasim Shah, and Md. Fouad Bin Amin. "Prospects of Poverty Elimination through Potential Zakat Collection in OIC-Member Countries: Reappraised." *Journal of Islamic Economics, Banking and Finance* 6, no. 3 (2010): 55–74.

Siddiqi, Muhammad Nejatullah. *Economics: An Islamic Approach.* Islamabad, Pakistan: Institute of Policy Studies/Islamic Foundation, 2001.

Smith, Adam. *An Inquiry into the Nature and Causes of the Wealth of Nations.* 2 vols. London: W. Strahan and T. Cadell, 1776.

———. *The Theory of Moral Sentiments, or, An Essay towards an Analysis of the Principles by Which Men Naturally Judge Concerning the Conduct and Character, First of Their Neighbors, and Afterwards of Themselves.* London: Printed for Andrew Millar, in the Strand; and Alexander Kincaid and J. Bell, in Edinburgh, 1759.

as-Sufi, Abdalqadir. "The Islamic Dinar—A Way-Stage Passed," Shaykh Dr. Abdalqadir as-Sufi (website). February 11, 2014. https://shaykhabdalqadir.com/2014/02/11/the-islamic-dinar-a-way-stage-passed/.

al-Ta'wīl, Muḥammad. "Zakat on Cash and Its Latest Developments: Why Silver Should Be the Basis for Appraising Zakat on Paper Money." Translated by Abdullah bin Ḥamīd ʿAlī. Lamppost Productions, 2011. https://lamppostedu.org/wp-content/uploads/2018/06/Zakat-on-Paper-Money.pdf.

al-Tirmidhi, Imām Abu 'Isa Muhammad. *Jami al-Tirmidhi.* https://sunnah.com/tirmidhi/about.

———. *Jami' al-Tirmidhi.* Damascus & Riyadh: Dar al-Fayha & Dar al-Salam, 1999.

Tomass, Mark. "Al-Maqrízi's *Book of Aiding the Nation by Investigating the Depression* of 1403–6: Translation and Commentary." In *Joseph A. Schumpeter, Historian of Economics: Selected Papers from the History of Economics Society Conference, 1994,* edited by Laurence S. Moss, 110–54. Perspectives on the History of Economic Thought. London: Routledge, 1996.

Vadillo, Umar. *Fatwa Concerning the Islamic Prohibition on Using Paper Money as a Medium of Exchange.* Granada, Spain: Madinah, 1991.

Yusuf, S. M. *Economic Justice in Islam.* New Delhi: Kitab Bhavan, 1988.

CPSIA information can be obtained
at www.ICGtesting.com
Printed in the USA
JSHW020154060622
26717JS00003B/12